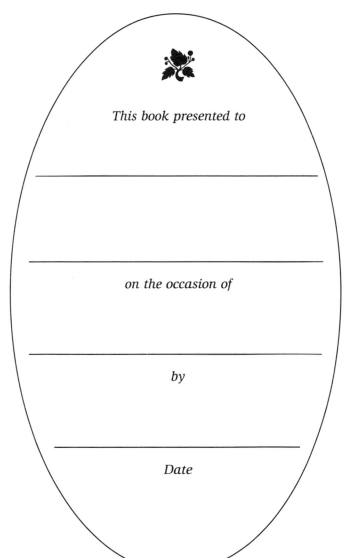

This book presented to

_____

_____

on the occasion of

_____

by

_____

Date

Meditations
from a
Mother's Heart

DAILY GRACE FOR MOTHERS

Pamela J. Kennedy

CPH
SAINT LOUIS

1   2   3   4   5   6   7   8   9   10   09 08 07 06 05 04 03 02 01 00

For my husband, Kraig,
who blessed our children with the love
from a father's heart.

Contents

Mothers from the Old Testament

Mothers from the New Testament

Mothers
from the
Old Testament

Eve

The First Mother

I AM EVE—CREATED, NOT BORN. When the earth was very young, the Lord God made Adam from the soil and breathed life into him. God said Adam was good and placed him in a perfect garden teeming with trees and flowers, vines and fruit. Adam walked with animals and birds and swam with fish and turtles. God brought all the creatures He had made before Adam to see what he would call them, and Adam named them all. But there was sadness in Adam's heart for even though he had the fellowship of the other created beings, he found no suitable helper among them. There was no one with whom he could share his thoughts and dreams, no one to lie down with in the cool evenings or to awaken with in the brightness of the morning. God saw this lack in Adam's life, and He knew just what to do.

God caused Adam to fall into a deep sleep and, while he was sleeping, opened his side and from a place near Adam's heart, removed a rib. After closing up the opening, God fashioned me from the flesh and bone of Adam, breathing His own life into me as He had the man. Then He brought me to Adam there in the garden, and Adam named me Woman, Eve, Life-Giver. God brought us together, and we became one, flesh and bone in unity of love and purpose before our Maker.

Together we walked and talked, tended the garden, and conversed with God. It was Paradise. Then one day I walked alone. I listened to a voice that was neither my husband's nor my Father's, and I was seduced into believing I could be something more than I was. How easy it seemed to swallow the lie and easier still to share the lie with Adam. Suddenly we knew we were wrong. By going our own way, we left the path of obedience and pure joy. In our shame we hid from God.

Driven by mercy and love, Father God searched for us and found us. His grace provided us with a covering, but His justice required us to leave the garden. Now we could no longer enjoy the sinless perfection of Eden. We must work for each day's meal, labor to bring forth fruit, and in the end we will know death.

But in the midst of our desolation and brokenness, God gave us the promise of a restored relationship through His Son—a Son who would lift all wounded spirits and wash away the stain of sin.

And when God gave us Cain, our first son, I knew that He had not withheld His blessings from us. Then Abel was born. But our children too were stained with sin. Soon anger and jealousy drove the elder to murder the younger. My mother's heart was broken with grief, and I suddenly understood how deeply I had grieved my Father in the garden. In later years God answered my prayers and sent another son, Seth, in place of Abel, the son Cain killed. Through Seth God would bring the Promised One; the One who would right all wrongs, vanquishing sin and death.

I was the first woman, but only one of many to come. I was beloved of God and of my husband. Although I was created in perfection I did not live perfectly, yet God in His goodness protected and provided for me. As I walked the earth I came to understand His mercy is everlasting and His love knows no bounds. ❦

Created by God

So God created man in His own image,
in the image of God He created him;
male and female He created them.
Genesis 1:27

Counselor, doctor, teacher, chef, taxi driver, police officer—who am I? A mother fills so many roles each day. Is it any wonder she wonders?

In the beginning, the very first mother may have had identity questions too. Perhaps that is why God takes the time to be very specific in the first chapter of Genesis. Three times in verse 27 the term "created" is used to define the origin of humankind. Created— not hatched, found, spontaneously generated, not evolved nor accidentally discovered. By a conscious decision of God we each were created; you and I and every mother who ever lived.

What a wonderful truth to grasp at those moments when doubts about self-worth nibble at the edges of my confidence. On days when my family's demands threaten to drown my identity, I take courage from the knowledge that I was personally created by God. Just like Eve, I bear the unmistakable stamp of my Maker. And because He made me, He knows me inside and out. I need not fear a loss of identity. I need only look into my heavenly Father's face to truly know who I am.

Scripture for Further Meditation:
Know that the L<small>ORD</small> *is God. It is He who made us, and we are His; we are His people, the sheep of His pasture. Psalm 100:3*

𝒫rayer:

Dear God, when I feel overwhelmed and under-appreciated, help me to remember that You made me by Your creative power and love. May I reflect Your image in attitudes, words, and actions today. In Jesus' name. Amen.

Created to Fulfill a Need

So the man gave names to all the livestock, the birds of the air and all the beasts of the field. But for Adam no suitable helper was found. Genesis 2:20

Haven't we all at times wondered, "Why am I here?" Everyone in the family might have a different answer if asked why Mom is around, but each person's response would probably involve a service she provides. She's here to cook and do the laundry. She picks me up from school and takes me to baseball (or soccer, or dance class, or piano lessons). She listens to my problems. She's my friend. She provides an income. Sometimes it feels as if everyone owns a piece of us and we exist only to serve. Is this what God intended when He said woman was created to be a "suitable helper"?

Looking back at the context of the Genesis passage, it's apparent that during the creative process God paraded all living creatures before Adam. At the end of that display, Adam realized there was no one to complement himself. He was alone, unfulfilled, incomplete. Adam needed a helper. I don't believe that helper was intended only to help in the garden or haul water from the river—several of the animals could have fulfilled those chores. No, he needed someone with whom he could communicate in thought and word. Created in the image of God, Adam possessed qualities the animals lacked, and none of them could meet his deepest needs. To be a helper under these circumstances is a high privilege, not a demeaning chore. It means my husband and my children are incomplete without the special insights and gifts God gave me to offer them. I have the opportunity to enrich my family as I submit to God's plan of being a "suitable helper." At times this may mean assisting in practical ways, but it also implies I have other things of value to contribute.

As I study God's Word and commune with Him, He shows me how I may best help my family. It may be offering discipline to a disobedient child. Another time it might involve sharing an insight or opinion during a decision-making time with my husband. It could mean learning a new skill in order to run the home more efficiently. Each day holds a variety of opportunities to expand the role of helper in the lives of those I love. Being a helper doesn't imply a role of lesser importance or of little value. On the contrary, it means being uniquely created to fulfill a need that could be met by no one else!

Scripture for Further Meditation:
I lift up my eyes to the hills—where does my help come from? My help comes from the LORD, the Maker of heaven and earth.
Psalm 121:1–2

Prayer:

Dear Jesus, please give me Your vision of my role in this family. Help me to be a suitable helper to my husband and children, bringing out the best in each and reflecting Your love in all I say and do. For Your name's sake. Amen.

Totally Naked

The man and his wife were both naked,
and they felt no shame. Genesis 2:25

Integrity, total honesty, and humility are qualities often discussed in classes on marriage and family life. Most of us, however, would prefer to talk about them rather than serve as examples of them. It is often frightening to think about having our thoughts and motives exposed because we know they are rarely pure. While we might present a respectable patina, scratch the surface of most of us and you quickly discover a tangle of selfishness, ambition, and pride. We'd be ashamed to be seen as we really are, and so we become masters of disguise.

The picture of Adam and Eve presented in Genesis at this point is one of pristine purity. I suspect their nakedness extended far beyond the physical. Each could look into the eyes of the other and see only truth. No thoughts were hidden, no ideas masked, no motives disguised. And when they walked and talked with God in the cool of the evenings, their conversations were devoid of unspoken agendas. Because of this they could truly know—and be known.

Many of us long to have our husbands and children truly know and understand us, but we constantly cover up our feelings, refusing to be honest in return. We play the martyr, saying, "It doesn't matter. I don't really mind," when things do matter and we mind very much. Some of us act like confident Christians while inside we're riddled with doubts and fears. We go from day to day with smiles on our faces, hiding the sadness in our hearts. Is it any wonder we feel misunderstood and alone?

If we wish to be known, we need to become knowable. For some of us it will be as uncomfortable as being physically naked because we are not used to showing others who we really are. For some a good place to begin is at a couples or family retreat where professionals offer guidance into appropriate methods of communicating. For others, a quiet walk together in the evening can provide a comfortable context for sharing openly. Developing a habit of spending time together alone allows husbands and wives to establish a level of trust that removes the fear from being emotionally naked. Just like Adam and Eve in that perfect garden, we can stand before one another in total honesty and feel no shame.

Scripture for Further Meditation:
Read Psalm 15

 *Prayer:*

Father, help me to develop honest relationships. Grant me wisdom to express the truth with love and to be willing to hear it as well. In Jesus' name. Amen.

Tempting Fruit

*When the woman saw that the fruit
of the tree was good for food and pleasing
to the eye, and also desirable for gaining
wisdom, she took some and ate it. She also
gave some to her husband, who was with her,
and he ate it. Genesis 3:6*

Things were going along perfectly well in the
Garden of Eden until one day when the traveling
salesman Serpent arrived. His sales pitch was clever
and seductive. Instead of pointing out all the advan-
tages and privileges available to Eve, he focused
immediately upon the one thing she lacked. His
finely rehearsed speech began by planting some
seeds of doubt. Then he watered the seeds with a lie
and before long, the tendrils of dissatisfaction
worked their way into Eve's thoughts. The fruit of
disobedience was ripe for picking before she even
realized it.

To some of us this seems just a quaint story from
Sunday school. But for others, it's a story that
repeats itself in our own homes on a daily basis. We
look around at our own personal "gardens" and
don't see the blessings there. Instead, we listen to the
voices of the salespeople who sow seeds of doubt in
our minds. "Surely you'd be happier if your husband
were more like that handsome character on your
favorite daytime drama." "This genuine imitation

diamond in a solid silver setting is only going to be available for 20 more minutes at this reduced price." "You deserve a better house, in a better neighborhood—and we can offer you a loan if you'll call now!"

Before long, dissatisfaction sets in and we, like Eve, begin to concentrate on the salesperson's goods instead of God's provision. We believe we would be more fulfilled if we were in a different relationship, had additional possessions, or lived in more desirable surroundings. And when that belief takes hold, the behavior of disobedience isn't far behind.

The world is filled with temptations offered by seductive salespeople whose interest is not our fulfillment, but their own. On that count, things haven't changed much from the days of Adam and Eve. Like Eve, we have an opportunity to listen to and obey God or believe the words of deceivers. It may not be easy to shut our ears to the constant barrage of voices in print and on television telling us what we need. Doing so, however, will help us hear the still small voice of our Father who promises to provide for all our needs beyond what we could think or ask. As women, we have a powerful influence on our husbands and children. The choice is ours. Like Eve, we can share our stolen fruit with those closest to us, spreading our discontent, or, by the Spirit's power, we can give thanks and praise to God by finding contentment in what His love has provided.

Scripture for Further Meditation:
I know what it is to be in need, and I know
what it is to have plenty. I have learned
the secret of being content in any and every
situation, whether well fed or hungry, whether
living in plenty or in want. I can do everything
through Him who gives me strength.
Philippians 4:12–13

Prayer:

Dear Lord, give me eyes to see the blessings
You have given me and ears to hear Your
voice. When other voices try to distract me,
let me lean on Your strength to remain faith-
ful to You. Thank You for providing all I need.
In Jesus' holy name. Amen.

Don't Blame Me!

Then the LORD God said to the woman,
"What is this you have done?" The woman
said, "The serpent deceived me, and I ate."
Genesis 3:13

"It isn't like I lied to someone, I just exaggerated on
the claim form. After all, everyone knows the insur-

ance companies have millions in excess premiums!"

"If these kids weren't so difficult to deal with, I wouldn't lose my temper and yell so much."

"Sure, I've let myself go, but look at my husband! He hasn't kept his youthful physique either."

Do any of these excuses sound familiar? When we fail to control ourselves, do or say things we know we shouldn't, or behave in ways that make us ashamed, most of us are quick to assign blame anywhere but on our own shoulders. In this way we are very much Eve's daughters.

As soon as we can find an excuse for our sin, we no longer feel so guilty. After all, if someone or something else is at fault, I can still feel pretty good about myself. And who has more reasons to blame than mothers? We're often overworked and under-rested, expected to know everything and accomplish any task with flair.

The problem with blaming is that it not only justifies bad behavior, it also perpetuates it. How can I hope to change if I don't even acknowledge I need to change? Looking at Eve, we recognize that her statement was basically true—the serpent did deceive her and she did eat. What she implies, however, is that the serpent's deception was the cause of her disobedience. In fact, the cause of her disobedience was her decision to believe the serpent instead of God and her choice to give in to temptation instead of remaining true to God's instruction. God has given me a free will to make the same kinds of decisions and choices today.

God instructs me to conduct business with honesty, to speak in love, to take care of my body. Because I am His child, I can follow His instructions or not. It is a choice God has given me. If I am to be the woman God intends, however, I need to stop blaming others when I fall short of God's demands and must suffer the consequences. Taking responsibility for my own sins is a vital step on the way to maturity as a believer. And as the Holy Spirit works faith in me, I am able to confess my sins, knowing that the blood of Jesus cleanses me and makes me right with God again.

Scripture for Further Meditation:
*He who conceals his sins does not prosper,
but whoever confesses and renounces them
finds mercy. Proverbs 28:13*

Prayer:

*Dear heavenly Father, help me to act
and speak in accordance with Your
will. Give me the courage to accept the
responsibility for my own sins and to seek
Your forgiveness for Jesus' sake so I may
mature as Your child and be a blessing
to my family. In Jesus' name. Amen.*

A Life-Giving Mother

Adam named his wife Eve, because she
would become the mother of all the living.
Genesis 3:20

The name Eve means living. What an appropriate name for a mother. Certainly a mother who carries a child in her womb for nine months can be said to give that child life in a very real sense. But a foster mother or an adoptive mother is just as life-giving as she pours herself into the little one God has entrusted to her. All mothers should be in the business of giving life to their children.

How do we do this? We care for them physically and thus help their bodies grow strong and healthy. We see to it that they eat well-balanced meals, bathe regularly, and have appropriate clothing for the weather they encounter. Emotionally we give them life by transmitting healthy attitudes, encouraging them to develop their personalities, and training them to restrain destructive behaviors. Spiritually we transmit life to our children when we teach them they are unique, valued, and redeemed by God; that God has a plan for their lives; and that they are His own dear children through the suffering, death, and resurrection of His only Son Jesus Christ.

But we cannot effectively transmit what we do not know and model ourselves. As tempting as it is at times to say, "Do as I say, not as I do!" what we *do* speaks many times louder than what we say. Our children will imitate us whether we want them to or not.

In order to be a life-giving mother, then, I must be careful to live a life-giving life. I cannot ask my children to take care of their bodies unless I first take care of my own. If I'm engaging in habits that are unhealthy, I can ask God to help me break them. If my conversation is filled with negativity and my attitude is one of complaint; if I constantly nag and criticize my children, how can I hope to build them up emotionally? If I'm not sure what I believe, if I've never taken time for Bible study, prayer, or worship, I cannot hope to introduce my sons and daughters to God. It would be like introducing them to a stranger!

It is exciting to realize the great privilege I have of giving life to my children as they grow. It is even more wonderful to recognize that God desires to be my partner in this enterprise. He promises to provide springs of living water, so I will have a life-giving abundance to share. What a joy to be an Eve—a mother who gives life!

Scripture for Further Meditation:
Whoever believes in Me, as the Scripture has said, streams of living water will flow from within him. John 7:38

Prayer:

Father, I desire to be a source of life in my family. Please give me wisdom as I help my children to grow physically, emotionally, and spiritually. Thank You for Your promise to fill me with living water through Jesus Christ. In His name. Amen.

Clothed by God

The LORD God made garments of skin for Adam and his wife and clothed them.
Genesis 3:21

After Adam and Eve disobeyed God and realized they were naked, they quickly fashioned garments of leaves to cover themselves. I suspect they were fairly pleased with how they solved their clothing problem. Pleased that is, until God showed up. In the clarity of God's revealing light, they realized how inadequate their own efforts were. How foolish and ashamed they must have felt as God told them of the consequences of their sin. Standing there in the midst of God's purity, their leafy togs looked ridiculous. So did God mock them and ridicule their clumsy attempt at a cover-up? No, instead He provided garments of skin, graphically demonstrating that only He can give us what we need.

As mothers we are often tempted to take things into our own hands, to handle situations quickly and get on to the next crisis. We do the best we can with what we have. I have found, however, that when I try to muddle through a difficult situation on my own or solve a perplexing problem by my wits alone, things often end up worse instead of better. I may only know one side of the story. I might misinterpret a conversation. My facts could be incorrect. My motives may be guided by personal interest instead of fairness. For any number of reasons, the "fig leaf" solutions I fashion are often inadequate.

How comforting to know that the Lord is always present and available to help me and provide exactly what I need to meet each situation I face as a mother. He knows my weaknesses and can turn them into strength. He understands my fears and can give me courage. He sees my limited insights and desires to grant me wisdom. In other words, God is anxious to clothe me with His garments of righteousness. He has made them available to me through Jesus. All I need to do is ask.

When a child comes home from school upset with a teacher or classmate and I am tempted to dash to the school in defensive anger, I should ask to be clothed with Christ's humility instead of my pride.

When I am emotionally exhausted by the demands of young children, a job, and housework, I need to seek rest in Christ instead of release through an ugly outburst. If I'm feeling unfulfilled at home, I can draw closer to God, discovering His purpose for me as revealed in His Word, instead of turning to unhealthy relationships or mindless fantasies. Just as God provided exactly what Eve needed, He is able to meet my every need as well. After all, He created me and knows what fits me best!

Scripture for Further Meditation:
Finally, be strong in the Lord and in His mighty power. Put on the full armor of God so that you can take your stand against the devil's schemes. Ephesians 6:10

Prayer:

Thank You, Jesus, for providing Yourself as a covering for my sin. Please help me to remember to consult You instead of turning to my own limited resources. Let me be a mother who is clothed with Your grace and mercy in every situation. Amen.

With the Lord's Help

Adam lay with his wife Eve, and she
conceived and gave birth to Cain.
She said, "With the help of the LORD
I have brought forth a man."
Genesis 4:1

What a miracle life is! From the first moment when sperm and egg unite until the day, some nine months later, when a child is born, the hand of God is evident. Science alone cannot explain the interweaving of cells and enzymes with intellect and emotion. Brain and bone and breath all come together in a symphony of order that defies analysis. Despite our abilities to build machines that seem to reason and to clone sheep and mice, to operate on unborn babies and to scan the inner workings of the heart, at the moment of birth we can only stand in awe. It is only with the help of the Lord that new life enters the world.

During pregnancy and often afterwards, a mother's body experiences myriad changes. We are bombarded with hormones that reshape our emotions just as the child growing within us reshapes our body. We may cry or laugh when we least expect to and become a total mystery to the husband who thought he knew us so well. Favorite foods send us dashing for the bathroom and sudden cravings drive us to the fridge at midnight. Is it any wonder we need extra help from the Lord to get through it all?

When Eve says, "With the help of the LORD I have brought forth a man," I don't think she's speaking only of the process of birth. I'll wager she was talking about the morning sickness, the swollen ankles, about sleepless nights, and sending Adam out for more olives. It must have been a frightening experience for her. She had no mother to comfort her and tell her all this was normal. She couldn't get advice from her aunts or sisters or friends. There was only Adam and he was probably as clueless as she! I suspect Eve developed a close relationship with the Lord during her pregnancy, depending upon Him to meet her needs.

As modern mothers we can take comfort in the knowledge that the Lord who was there for Eve is also here with us. Times and the world may have changed, but the Creator of both has not. He is able to uphold and sustain you and me just as He did the very first mother. And when we hold our own newborn, we can echo her words in wonder: "With the help of the Lord I have brought forth this child."

Scripture for Further Meditation:
For You created my inmost being;
You knit me together in my mother's womb.
I praise You because I am fearfully and
wonderfully made; Your works are wonderful,
I know that full well. Psalm 139:13–14

Prayer:

I praise You, Father, for the miracle of new life. Thank You that You are always willing to help me with this precious child You've placed in my keeping. May I always remember she (he) is Yours, not mine. In Your holy name. Amen.

Sarah

Chosen to Be a Princess

I AM SARAH, BUT THAT WAS NOT ALWAYS MY NAME. My parents named me Sarai and pledged me in marriage to Abram, son of Terah. Although I could not bear children, my husband's love remained strong and true, and we planned to live out our quiet lives in the land of the Chaldeans. And then, one day, at an age when most women are grandmothers, my life took a very unexpected turn.

My husband heard a message from the Lord, telling him to leave our country and go to a different land where Abram would become a great nation and a blessing to all peoples. It was an amazing revelation, for we had no children and didn't even know where God was sending us. Yet we chose to trust, packed up our belongings, bade farewell to loved ones, and followed the leading of God.

The traveling was difficult, and there were dangers all along the way. When famine struck, we fled to Egypt for food and protection. There, disguised as Abram's sister, I lived for a time within the palace walls. When Pharaoh discovered our ruse, he angrily cast us out, and we fled to the desert regions of the Negev. There we were blessed with prosperity and abundance, but still Abram felt the hand of God leading him on. Year after year we wandered until my husband found a place of peace near Bethel—the house of God. There we parted company with our nephew, Lot, who left our hillside pastures for the rich valleys of Sodom and Gomorrah.

We ceased traveling, but my heart remained unsettled. God's promise to Abram for a son and countless heirs was blocked by my barrenness. Night after night I tossed upon my bed, searching for a solution to our dilemma. Alone in the darkness I recalled an ancient custom of our people. If Abram were to father a child with my handmaid, I could claim the child as my own. It seemed a good plan, and I soon convinced Abram to accede to my wishes. What followed, however, was not what I had expected.

Hagar, my Egyptian servant, did conceive and bear a child by my husband. But Ishmael's birth did not bring the blessings I had envisioned. Instead, hatred and jealousy took root in our home. For 13 years bitterness was my daily food as Hagar and her son taunted me. Then, in Abram's 99th year, the Lord appeared, renewing His vow and changing my husband's name to Abraham—father of a multitude. I was given a new name as well: Sarah—a princess. But even more wonderful was the fact that God had not forgotten me, nor punished me for running ahead of His plan. In His grace and mercy I was to bear a son! The very thought of it made me laugh out loud. In fact, when the child was born, less than a year later, we named him Isaac—he laughs!

What joy our son brought to us. Each day as I held and nursed him, I blessed the Lord for granting our hearts' desire. But as Isaac grew, the old rivalries increased until I feared for our little son's life. I knew Hagar and Ishmael must be sent away, but it grieved my husband to think of losing his older son. Again God spoke and comforted Abraham with the promise of a heritage for Ishmael.

With our antagonists gone, we thought our troubles were ended, but we soon learned the Lord was not finished with His plan for us. One day He challenged Abraham's obedience with an awful test. He requested the sacrifice of our beloved son on the mountain of Moriah. Steadfast, yet filled with dread, Abraham took our precious Isaac to the place of burnt offerings. There, in humility and obedience, my husband prepared to offer our only son to the only God.

As the knife blade flashed in the sun, the angel of the Lord stopped the sacrifice and provided a ram instead. Then the word of the Lord came to my dear Abraham, reaffirming His promises.

I lived to be 127 years old, and many considered me to be both wealthy and wise. Their assessment was not completely wrong. For though my human wisdom often failed me, the Lord enriched me with the knowledge of His truth. He taught me that obedience is far better than sacrifice, that God's strength is always available for those times when mine fails, and that I was truly a princess, not by birth, but because the King of Heaven chose me as His own. 🙢

Moving On

So Abram left, as the LORD had told him;
and Lot went with him. Abram was
seventy-five years old when he set out
from Haran. He took his wife Sarai,
his nephew Lot, all the possessions
they had accumulated and the people
they had acquired in Haran, and they
set out for the Land of Canaan, and
they arrived there. Genesis 12:4–5

Sarai had lived in Haran for most of her married
life. She had friends and family there, was well established in the community, and probably lived comfort-
ably in a fine home with her wealthy husband. Then
one day something unusual happened. Abram, her
husband, announced he had heard a message from
the Lord, and they were moving to Canaan. Aside
from the fact that none of them had ever been to
Canaan, the trip had other challenges. They were
traveling with lots of folks and tents and animals and
household goods. It was a long way from Haran to
Canaan and once they got there, they met with some
unfriendly residents and had to move on. First they
went to the hills between Bethel and Ai. Next they
traveled toward the Negev desert. Food was sparse
and they didn't linger long in the Negev region before
they were off to Egypt. After some unpleasantness
there, the extended family headed back again to

Negev, then from place to place before returning to the hills where they had lived before. It wasn't long, however, until they pulled up stakes again and moved on to Hebron where they finally settled near the great trees of Mamre.

All in all, they probably traveled more than 1,000 miles on foot. Sarai must have set up tentkeeping at least a dozen times during the years of their journeying—and she was no spring chicken! I can identify with Sarai. During my husband's 28-year career in the Navy, we moved 18 times. It can be discouraging to have to set up housekeeping over and over again, to put down roots knowing they will soon be uprooted. Sarai, no doubt, took comfort in knowing that the Lord was not limited to one place, but traveled with them wherever they went. His presence and care surrounded them, and so the first thing they did in each new home was to establish a family altar for prayer and worship.

Our world is constantly in motion, and few families stay in one place anymore. As mothers, it's easy to become frustrated when we must leave familiar friends, family, churches, and schools and move to new locations where we may not know anyone. At these times it is good to remember that our family tree has roots not in a place, but in a person: Jesus Christ. As we learn new routines and meet new friends, we have the comfort of knowing that our Savior is not only there with us, but has gone on ahead to make a way for us. He is more than able to help us adjust as individuals and as a family. When we trust our future to His keeping, He will do for us what He did for Sarai—delight us with His wonderful plans and promises.

Scripture for Further Meditation:
Jesus replied, "If anyone loves Me, he will obey My teaching. My Father will love him, and We will come to him and make Our home with him." John 14:23

Prayer:

Dear Jesus, thank You for making Your dwelling place within my heart. Help me to remember that my security is in You, not in a house or a hometown. If You call me to move, give me courage and contentment knowing You will always be with me no matter where I live. In Your name I pray. Amen.

Just Do It

Now Sarai, Abram's wife, had borne him no
children. But she had an Egyptian maidser-
vant named Hagar; so she said to Abram,
"The LORD has kept me from having children.
Go, sleep with my maidservant; perhaps I can
build a family through her." Genesis 16:1–2

Many years had passed since God first called Abram
to take his family and move to the land of promise.
Abram and Sarai had been faithful to go where God
directed them, but still they did not see the fulfillment
to the promise of a son. I'm sure as year after year
passed and Sarai remained barren, the prospect of a
child being born seemed more remote than ever. After
all, she and Abram were not getting any younger! It is
at this point that Sarai decides to take matters into her
own hands. She develops a plan to "help" God.

In accordance with the custom of the time, it was
permissible for a barren wife to give her maid to her
husband for the purpose of producing an heir. If the
maid gave birth to a child, that child could legally be
adopted by the husband and wife. It was a logical,
sensible, and lawful solution to Sarai's problem, and
she urged Abram to just do it.

Often, when we are tired of waiting for God, when
His answers are slow in coming and we see no solution to our dilemma, we are also tempted to just do
something. We look around for a logical way out of a

situation. Perhaps we search for a legal loophole or a practical way to solve our problem. Like Sarai, our solution may be perfectly acceptable to those around us, and it may even seem to accomplish the very thing we desire. The problem is that by acting on our own, apart from God's direction and outside of His plan, we often create new and more serious difficulties for ourselves and others.

God knows the end from the beginning. He understands where I need to grow through patience, perseverance, humility, and even disappointment. As the Lord of time, He also knows the perfect season for all things. Over and over in Scripture we read the phrase, "in the fullness of time." That's the point at which God moves. When I "just do it" instead of waiting for God's fullness of time, I place obstacles in my own path. Because of Sarai's plan, she endured insults and disharmony in her household. She mistreated another and caused her husband pain. All of this could have been avoided if she had believed the Lord and waited for His perfect timing. When I need to experience God's answers to my prayers, I can remember this lesson from Sarai and resist the urge to "just do it" myself.

Scripture for Further Meditation:
Commit your way to the Lord; trust in Him and He will do this: He will make your righteousness shine like the dawn, the justice of your cause like the noonday sun. Psalm 37:5–6

*Dear Father, when I am tempted to take
things into my own hands and to act without
Your direction, give me courage and faith
to wait upon You. Help me to listen for
Your voice and to live in accordance with
Your will. Thank You for Your promise
to direct my paths as I trust in You.
In Jesus' name. Amen.*

It's All Your Fault

*Then Sarai said to Abram, "You are
responsible for the wrong I am suffering.
I put my servant in your arms, and now
that she knows she is pregnant, she despises
me. May the L<small>ORD</small> judge between you and me."
Genesis 16:5*

Just a few verses earlier, we listen to Sarai con-
vince Abram to father a child by Hagar, the Egyptian
maid. When Hagar becomes pregnant, however,
things don't work out quite as Sarai had expected.
The expectant mother taunts her barren mistress and
Sarai decides the whole mess is Abram's fault! We

may wonder at Sarai's short memory or deliberate denial, but chances are, we can glimpse a bit of ourselves in her lament.

It is easy to take the credit when our idea for the school fund-raiser brings in thousands of dollars or the church production we direct is a smashing success. But what happens when no one attends the Bible study I organize or I make a presentation that bombs? Quickly I look for something or someone to blame. Usually it isn't too difficult. There are many who are eager to keep me from taking the moral high road. Billboards advertise attorneys who offer "no-fault divorce" or others who promise to get their clients off the hook for everything from drunk driving to murder. Pop-psychologists maintain bad behavior is the fault of parents, society, genes—even food additives. If we listen to the voices around us, we are all total innocents suffering at the hands of circumstances or others. But the result of accepting this no-fault mentality is moral bankruptcy.

If I am to be a woman of integrity, I cannot take the cheap and easy way out. I cannot avoid accepting responsibility when I blow it. I cannot shift the blame. Repentance is the pathway to forgiveness and restoration, but without responsibility, there can be no true repentance.

When I, like Sarai, willfully take control of situations and then experience the pain my poor decisions cause, I cannot receive healing by telling someone else, "It's your fault!" On the other hand, when I humbly accept responsibility for the results of my choices, I model spiritual maturity for my children and have an opportunity to grow as well. If my actions have caused another's pain, it is my duty as a Christian to go to him or her in humility, acknowledge my error and, with God's help, seek forgiveness and restoring love. It may not be the most comfortable way, but it is most certainly the best way.

Scripture for Further Meditation:
Blessed are they whose ways are blameless, who walk according to the law of the LORD. Psalm 119:1

Prayer:

Dear Lord, help me to keep Your words in my heart and mind so I will be always mindful of how You would have me choose. When I do act according to my own will, give me the humility to admit my fault and seek forgiveness. Help me to grow in wisdom, integrity, and trust in You as I become the woman You intend me to be. In Jesus' name. Amen.

Power Play

"Your servant is in your hands," Abram
said. "Do with her whatever you think best."
Then Sarai mistreated Hagar; so she fled
from her. Genesis 16:6

As the mistress of a household, Sarai possessed power. She had the power of influence with Abram, the power of giving or withholding favors, the power to minister to or mistreat her servants. Few modern mothers have household help, but we still have a great deal of power in our homes.

According to how I handle money, I have the power to build the financial security of my family or to run it into debt. My attention to meal preparations has an impact upon the eating habits and, eventually, the health of my family. When I choose methods of training and discipline for my children, I have the power to increase or tear down their emotional well-being. I have the power to point them toward God or to impede their spiritual growth through both my teaching and example. Sometimes I may not feel very powerful within the family, but in truth a mother has tremendous power.

Sarai was given free rein to exercise power in her situation with Hagar, and she decided to make Hagar's life miserable. She was so successful, the servant girl ran away from home, preferring the hostility of the desert to the constant mistreatment of her mistress.

We may argue that Hagar got what she deserved having made her contempt for Sarai so obvious, but Sarai was not only much older, she was also a woman of the covenant. As such she was called to a higher standard of behavior.

As Christian mothers we too are called to a higher standard of behavior. We are not to use the power given us in the family to harm, but to help. It is not always easy to refrain from lashing out in anger when we're frustrated or tired. Some of us need the Lord's strength to resist the temptation to yell, to use sarcasm or cutting words. But if we use the power granted to us by our wise heavenly Father to build up our children and husbands, to model fairness and mercy, then we channel our strength for good and for God's glory. Truly powerful mothers are those who submit their wills to Christ's and ask for the power of His Spirit to flow through them to their families.

Scripture for Further Meditation:
For God did not give us a spirit of timidity, but a spirit of power, of love and of self-discipline. 2 Timothy 1:7

*Thank You, Father, for placing me in
a position of power within my family.
Give me a heart of humility, and a willingness
to submit my words and actions to Your
authority so my family will be encouraged
to grow in an atmosphere of loving-kindness.
In Jesus' name. Amen.*

A New Name

*God also said to Abraham, "As for Sarai
your wife, you are no longer to call her Sarai;
her name will be Sarah." Genesis 17:15*

What shall we name the baby? From the time
pregnancy is confirmed, this is an important question
for most couples. Dozens of books have been written
offering suggestions, definitions, and consequences
of different names. Each year a list of "in" and "out"
names is published, so new parents might choose a
title for Jr. more wisely. In Scripture, much thought
was also given to names. In fact, some names were
even changed by the Lord to indicate a new purpose
or plan for a person's life. Abram was renamed

Abraham, Jacob was renamed Israel (Genesis 32:28) and Simon was renamed Peter (Matthew 16:18).

In this verse, God declares Sarai will be called Sarah. It doesn't seem like much of a change, does it? What's one letter more or less? The name, Sarai, meant *my princess*; that is the princess belonging to Abraham. Sarah, however, means *princess*. It's a more inclusive name and indicates that Sarah's role as the mother of Abraham's long-awaited son was not to be just a blessing to her husband and family, but a blessing for all who would come after her. God had unlimited expectations and opportunities for Sarah that she couldn't even imagine!

Wouldn't it be exciting to have God give you a new name that carried with it the promise of unlimited blessings? Scripture teaches us that when the Lord makes us His children through His gift of water and the Word, this is exactly what happens! "I will give them an everlasting name that will not be cut off" (Isaiah 56:5b). Our new name identifies us as no longer belonging only to ourselves or our family, but as daughters of the Living God. We have a plan and purpose designed by our Lord and an opportunity to be a blessing far beyond the confines of our own earthly family.

Sometimes as mothers it is easy to become bogged down in the daily details of life. At times just getting through the day at hand seems blessing enough! But I believe God is asking us to answer to a new name, a new significance, as members of His family. When we see ourselves as daughters of the King of heaven, not just as someone's mom, we begin to grasp the wonderful opportunities God has for us. Ask the Lord to help you discover ways to expand your influence for Him beyond the confines of your own home. In doing so you will experience the joy of having a new name.

Scripture for Further Meditation:
Do not rejoice that the spirits submit to you, but rejoice that your names are written in heaven. Luke 10:20

Prayer:

Dear Father, thank You that because You have made me Your child through Jesus, You have given me a new name as a member of Your family. Help me to keep in mind that I live not only for myself, but also for You. May I always bring blessing to Your name. Amen.

No Laughing Matter

So Sarah laughed to herself as she
thought, "After I am worn out and my
master is old, will I now have this pleasure?"
Then the LORD said to Abraham, "Why did
Sarah laugh and say, 'Will I really have
a child, now that I am old?' Is anything too
hard for the LORD? I will return to you
at the appointed time next year and
Sarah will have a son." Genesis 18:12–14

I am nowhere near 90 years old, but I can strongly identify with Sarah at this point. My husband and I were married for nine years before our first child was born and during those years there were many times when I laughed, not with joy, but derision at the prospect of ever giving birth to a child. After so many infertility procedures, dashed hopes, and unrealized dreams, it seemed ridiculous to even imagine it. Years later, however, I look back in wonder and echo God's words to Abraham, "Is anything too hard for the LORD?"

When we are in the midst of what seems an impossible situation, it is easy to become overwhelmed and discouraged. What should we do about a strong-willed toddler who refuses to eat or go to bed or behave? How can we deal with a disease or accident threatening the life of our child? When a teenager defies authority and engages in destructive actions, what should we do? How can we reach the heart of a child who declares he has rejected God? There are situations beyond our control crowding into every aspect of parenting. At times they so overwhelm us that we believe there are no solutions and that we are helpless and hopeless. We laugh, not in delight, but in utter disbelief that things will ever change for the better.

At these times it is good to be reminded that God is never overwhelmed or without hope. Nothing is too difficult for Him. His purposes are established and at the appointed time will be accomplished. Where does that leave us as mothers then? It gives us an amazing opportunity to participate with God through the privilege of prayer. Over and over in Scripture, God promises to accomplish great things for His children when they pray in accordance with His will. As we bring our "impossible" parenting situations to God, we can tap into His wisdom and peace. We can ask Him to direct us to His solution to our dilemma. By seeking to learn what He wants to accomplish through these difficult times, we can pray in accordance with His will. If we choose to fret, worry, nag, and complain, we will continue to see only the impossibility of our circumstances. It's when we view things from God's perspective that we realize our problems are no laughing matter to God, but serious opportunities to reveal His power.

Scripture for Further Meditation:
I tell you the truth, anyone who has faith in Me will do what I have been doing. He will do even greater things than these, because I am going to the Father. And I will do whatever You ask in My name, so that the Son may bring glory to the Father. You may ask Me for anything in My name, and I will do it. John 14:12–14

Prayer:

Dear Lord, it is easy to look at my problems and think of them as impossibilities. Help me to submit each situation to You in prayer. I believe that nothing is impossible for You and I desire to see Your will accomplished in my life. Thank You for the opportunity to experience Your presence daily. Amen.

You Promised!

Now the LORD was gracious to Sarah as He had said, and the LORD did for Sarah what He had promised. Sarah became pregnant and bore a son to Abraham in his old age, at the very time God had promised him. Genesis 21:1–2

Today promises don't seem to mean as much as they used to. People often tell others what they think will please them instead of the truth. Or they make promises without any intention of fulfilling them. When it comes time to deliver on a promise, excuses abound: I was too busy or tired. I forgot. I just can't. It's not convenient now.

Thank the Lord He does not treat us as we treat one another! Scripture reminds us over and over that God is a keeper of promises. In the above text, we read of the fulfillment of one of God's promises to Abraham and Sarah. By carefully reading these short verses, we catch a glimpse of how and why God is the perfect promise keeper.

First of all, note that "the Lord was gracious." God doesn't keep His promises out of obligation or because we are deserving. He keeps them because of His grace. In fact this indicates that God has no obligation to us and we are totally undeserving. That's what grace is all about—God giving us what we don't deserve. Sarah had done nothing to earn the right to have a child. In fact, she had laughed at the prospect! But God, in His grace, promised to give her the desires of her heart.

Second, God did "as He had said." God's promises are a fulfillment of His word. When God speaks, He always speaks truth. If I want to know more about God's promises to me as a believer, I can listen to Him as He speaks to me through Scripture, the wise counsel of mature Christians, and in prayer as He and I communicate together. And then I need to believe that what He has said is true.

Third, "the LORD did for Sarah what He had promised." God's promises result in action. When I take God's promises for my own and wait for His fulfillment, He will act. Often, however, His actions may not be those I expect. As I claim His promise to draw others to Himself, I may find He wishes to use me to share the Good News and I thus become instrumental in His promise keeping. When I depend upon His promise to heal me, I may discover He provides an eternal healing for my heart and wounded spirit, instead of the physical healing I anticipated. While we can be sure that God acts upon His promises, we recognize that His ways are not always our ways.

As mothers, we know we may not always fulfill the promises we make to our own children, but we can be sure that because of His grace toward us in Jesus Christ, God will perfectly fulfill His promises to us in both word and deed.

Scripture for Further Meditation:
Your kingdom is an everlasting kingdom,
and Your dominion endures through all
generations. The LORD is faithful to all His
promises and loving toward all He has made.
Psalm 145:13

Prayer:

Father, I thank You that Your word is truth and that You always keep Your promises. Help me not only to trust You more, but also to be a trustworthy woman. Give me a desire to speak the truth in love and to be gracious in making and keeping my promises to others. Amen.

Rebekah

Comforter and Conniver

I AM REBEKAH, DAUGHTER OF BETHUEL, Abraham's nephew. I lived in a small town with my family, closely protected by loving relatives. Our lives were directed by the seasons and the crops, but my heart longed for adventure outside the hills surrounding our village. Little did I know that my prayers would become reality.

It was a hot afternoon in the city of Nahor, but it was my favorite time of day. I hurried out to meet the other young women in the town as we congregated on our way to fetch water. Eagerly we chattered, laughing and teasing one another as usual. Nearing the spring, I spied a well-dressed stranger. I knew not to stare at him, but we rarely had such interesting visitors and it was difficult not to take a peek or two as I filled my water jar. When I turned to leave, the man spoke, asking me for a drink. Quickly I lowered the jar and poured a cup of cool water for the stranger. Then, noting the thirsty glances of the camels tethered nearby, I offered to fill the watering trough. The man observed me silently as I watered the beasts, and I wondered if he was displeased with my boldness. But when I finished the task, he smiled warmly. Then, quite to my surprise, he presented me with a gold nose ring and two bracelets and inquired about my family asking if he and his entourage might spend the night at our home! My ordinary trip to the well had turned into an intriguing adventure!

Within hours, I was given beautiful gifts and a proposal of marriage from the stranger's wealthy master. Dismissing my family's pleas to delay, I quickly accepted the visitor's offer to leave immediately. In my heart, I trusted that God was answering my secret prayers.

The first time I saw my dear husband, Isaac, he was meditating in a field shimmering with starlight. As he approached our caravan, I slipped to the ground and modestly drew my veil around me. Even through my veil I could tell Isaac was a man of strength and character. From the very beginning of our life together, I never regretted my choice to leave my parents' home.

We were husband and wife in every sense of the word, bound in heart and soul as well as body. In the cool evenings, Isaac spoke to me of his love for the

Lord and of Yahweh's plan to establish a people for His own. As the years passed, I grieved, for I was barren. Would Isaac take another wife to be the mother of his descendants? But dear, sweet Isaac assured me of his love and prayed for God to make me fruitful.

At last I became pregnant and the Lord revealed to me that I carried twins who would grow to be the fathers of two nations—nations that would war with one another. From birth, the Lord's prophecy was fulfilled. My sons, Esau and Jacob, were as different as day and night. They argued with each other constantly, and Isaac and I began to take sides; he with Esau and I with Jacob. The harmony of our home dissolved and as the boys grew, so did the distance between Isaac and me. More and more I looked to Jacob for comfort and understanding and when the time came for Isaac to bestow his blessing on our elder son, Esau, I hatched a plan to steal the honor for Jacob.

Far from bringing joy into our home, my plot exacted a terrible price. Esau's resentment toward Jacob escalated into plans for murderous revenge. Isaac's heart broke as his beloved Esau defied his wishes and married not one, but two pagan women. Jacob was forced to leave home to escape his brother's rage, and Isaac and I were divided by a wedge of distrust. My dreams lay shattered at my feet. I had selfishly asserted my own will and the price I paid was great. Although I lived for almost two decades after Jacob's departure, I never saw him again. 🌿

Let Me Help You

> *"Drink, my lord," she said, and quickly*
> *lowered the jar to her hands and gave him*
> *a drink. After she had given him a drink,*
> *she said, "I'll draw water for your camels too,*
> *until they have finished drinking." So she*
> *quickly emptied her jar into the trough,*
> *ran back to the well to draw more water,*
> *and drew enough for all his camels.*
> Genesis 24:18–20

I have a friend who has a knack for always seeing what needs to be done, doing it quickly, then adding some extra personal touches. She's such a joy! If she knows someone is going through a tough time, she doesn't wait for a call before offering to bring over dinner. Then she adds a special dessert and a handful of flowers from her garden as well. She's efficient and thoughtful, seeing beyond the obvious need and offering more than is expected.

Rebekah was that kind of woman too. When Abraham's servant requested a drink of water she looked beyond him to the tired, dusty camels waiting in the hot sun. Then she generously offered to fetch water for them as well. And notice, she didn't do her acts of hospitality reluctantly. Scripture says she "quickly" gave him a drink, "quickly" watered the camels, and "ran" back to the well for more water. And I expect she had to make several trips. Camels consume lots of water! She was eager and generous in her hospitality—a woman who found joy in serving.

As mothers and wives, we often are expected to entertain others or serve our family. Whenever this happens, our heart attitude is exposed. Are we resentful and reluctant when asked to give of ourselves? Or do we reflect Rebekah's enthusiasm to serve? As Christians we are called by the Savior to be servants. When we offer service with joy and enthusiasm, we not only bless others, but also bring glory to the Lord. For in the end, all acts of service are only a pale reflection of His loving and sacrificial service to us.

Scripture for Further Meditation:
You, my brothers, were called to be free.
But do not use your freedom to indulge
the sinful nature; rather, serve one another
in love. Galatians 5:13

Prayer:

Lord Jesus, develop in me the heart of a
servant. Help me to be willing to give my time
and energy to others with joy and enthusiasm
as a reflection of Your loving service to me.
Thank You for Your life of service on earth
so I might more clearly understand what it
means to serve You. Amen.

I Will Go

Then they said, "Let's call the girl and ask her about it." So they called Rebekah and asked her, "Will you go with this man?" "I will go," she said. Genesis 24:57–58

It's not always easy to change direction. We get used to the way we do things. There's comfort in the familiar and security in what we know. But then the Lord intrudes into our comfortable, orderly lives and offers us a new option. How do I respond when I discover I'm pregnant again, after I thought my family was just the right size? What is my reaction when faced with an unexpected move, a lost job, even a natural disaster that alters the course of my life? While I may not control such unexpected events, I do control how I choose to respond to them.

Rebekah is minding her own business one hot, dry day when a stranger comes to her home. He explains to her family how God has directed his path to their door and then continues to reveal how Rebekah's response to him is a direct answer to prayer. When the servant offers a marriage proposal on behalf of his master, Rebekah's family lobbies for more time. They hadn't planned on saying good-bye to their beloved daughter quite this soon. Eventually they determine to ask what Rebekah thinks. Notice how she responds. Despite the sudden and radical change of plans this proposal offers, she is convinced it is from

God and replies simply, "I will go."

In her answer we find obedience distilled into three words. Her family urges her to wait a while and go later, but she has no such reservations. She is willing to follow now.

When the Lord allows unexpected circumstances to enter my life, do I, like Rebekah, face them fearlessly, determined to walk on with God's hand leading me? Or do I hang back, clinging to my own plans, resentful or fearful of change?

If God goes before me, I need not fear what lies ahead. I can risk change. I can dare to take a new direction. I can follow Him to a future I never would have experienced otherwise.

Scripture for Further Meditation:
He guides me in paths of righteousness for His name's sake. Even though I walk through the valley of the shadow of death, I will fear no evil, for You are with me; Your rod and Your staff they comfort me. Psalm 23:3–4

Prayer:

Thank You, God, that You have plans for me that I can't even imagine. Help me to be attentive to Your voice so that when You call me to change direction in my life, I am prepared to answer, "I will go." In Jesus' name. Amen.

A Comforting Wife

Isaac brought her into the tent of his mother Sarah, and he married Rebekah. So she became his wife, and he loved her; and Isaac was comforted after his mother's death. Genesis 24:67

Are you a comforter? When everyone comes home at the end of the day is there a welcome waiting? I once attended a class on parenting and the instructor said, "If you want to know about the climate in your home, ask the members of your family what they feel when they place their hand on the doorknob to enter the house. Is it relief or dread; peace or anxiety?"

Sadly, the world isn't a very friendly place for families anymore. Careers demand more of our time. Business trips separate us for days or even weeks. Even at home, television, sports, music lessons, and school activities vie for our hours, pulling us away from one another. And yet, in the midst of it, we all long to find comfort—to be comforted.

After Sarah died, Isaac grieved deeply. He was busy tending the herds and managing the household servants for his father, but his heart was heavy. Then Rebekah arrived. She married Isaac, and the very first thing Scripture records about her as a wife is that she comforted her husband. Perhaps she listened to his recollections of Sarah. Perhaps her separation from her own parents caused her to express compassion and tenderness toward Isaac, filling the emptiness of his heart. However she did it, we know she found a way to provide much-needed comfort.

Being a comforter requires a willingness to listen and learn when our husbands and children are hurting. It demands the humility to place their needs above our own. Providing comfort doesn't always mean making a grand gesture, though. Sometimes small gestures of kindness, a blessing as they walk out the door, a note tucked in a lunch box or briefcase, a silly card, a hug, or special treat offers comfort to someone who feels overwhelmed with responsibility or under-appreciated. When we reach out to comfort others, we strengthen the fabric of our family and build encouragement into the walls of our home. As mothers and wives we have a wonderful opportunity to offer daily comfort to those we love.

Scripture for Further Meditation:
Praise be to the God and Father of our
Lord Jesus Christ, the Father of compassion
and the God of all comfort, who comforts
us in all our troubles, so that we can comfort
those in any trouble with the comfort we
ourselves have received from God.
2 Corinthians 1:3–4

 *Prayer:*

*Dear Lord Jesus, give me a spirit of
compassion that I might know how to
comfort my husband and children today.
May all I say and do reflect the love and
compassion I have received from You.
In Your name I pray. Amen.*

Prayer Partners

*Isaac prayed to the Lord on behalf of his wife,
because she was barren. The Lord answered
his prayer, and his wife Rebekah became
pregnant. Genesis 25:21*

The opportunity to pray for one's mate is a privilege as well as a responsibility. I must admit, however, that often my prayers for my husband center upon what it is I'd like God to do to or for my beloved so that my life will be easier! "Please Lord, let him spend less time in the garage working on his projects and more time with me." "In Your wisdom and grace, Lord, could You cause the TV to break down Monday night so we can have a conversation?" "Father, could You give him a holy nudge to be more active at church?" Somehow, I suspect these aren't the kinds of prayers God intends when He encourages us to pray for one another.

In the verse above, we see the key to the power of Isaac's prayer for Rebekah in the words, "on behalf of." Isaac wasn't praying for himself, nor was he praying for God to do something to Rebekah to make her husband's life more comfortable. Instead, he was going before God with his wife's needs uppermost and pleading for God to act in a way that she would find fulfillment. This is the prayer of love for one's spouse.

How do we pray on behalf of our husbands? First, we willingly set aside our own concerns and look at what concerns him. Is there a project at work, a business associate with a problem, a financial crisis looming, a health issue, or something else weighing on his mind? If he is not used to communicating his needs, you might ask, "What could I be praying for you today?" Second, we willingly pray for God to answer according to what is best for our husband in the situation. (Sometimes we pray for an answer we perceive as having the best outcome for us!) Third, we are diligent in prayer. Talking about praying, even having the best intentions to pray is not the same as actually spending time in prayer. Fourth, we realize that God is the one answering the prayer. It is not our place to nag or try to maneuver circumstances to bring about the response we see as desirable. Have faith that God, who loves our husbands even more than we do, will answer prayer as He has promised.

Bringing those we love before the throne of God in prayer is the right and privilege of our faith in Christ. What better way to strengthen our marriages than to pray diligently on behalf of our husbands?

Scripture for Further Meditation:
Devote yourselves to prayer, being watchful and thankful. Colossians 4:2

Prayer:

Thank You, God, for my husband. Give me a heart sensitive to understand his needs and to bring them to You in prayer. Bind the two of us together in the strength of Your love so we may truly be one in our devotion to Your will. In Jesus' name. Amen.

What's Going on, Lord?

The babies jostled each other within her, and she said, "Why is this happening to me?" So she went to inquire of the LORD. Genesis 25:22

Where do you go first when you can't figure out what's happening in your life? Do you call the psychic hotline? Do you dial up a friend? Do you run home to Mom? Or perhaps you're one of those women who tucks her doubts away and carries on as if nothing is bothering her. Each of these responses offers answers of one kind or another, but all fall short of producing the best solution to our quandaries.

Rebekah may not have been a very sophisticated woman with lots of biblical scholarship under her belt, but she knew where to go when she had a perplexing problem. She went directly to the Lord. She understood that God was inextricably intertwined with her life. She had seen His divine purpose in choosing her to be Isaac's wife. She had experienced the miracle of answered prayer as He opened her womb and she became pregnant. Looking at His faithfulness in the past, she knew He would neither forget nor forsake her in her present predicament. She fell on her knees before Him and poured out her concerns.

In the midst of a trial, it's sometimes easy to forget that God promises to be there for us. It seems easier to run to people we can see and touch. But others, however comforting, can only offer us help out of their limited resources. They only know what we tell them about our situation. They only understand with a finite mind. God, on the other hand, knows things about our problems that we don't even understand.

He is not blinded by ignorance or prejudice nor limited in any way. He knows, in addition, what lies ahead of us and how our current situation plays a part in our maturing and growth. Therefore, when we turn to Him, we avail ourselves of the very best help we could possibly receive. To be sure, He may not always reveal the purpose behind our trials immediately. His answers, when they come, may not be the ones we had hoped for or even anticipated. But His answers are always true and loving. And with or without an immediate resolution to our concerns, He brings peace.

When we are tossed by the waves of fear, confusion, and doubt, our Savior stands ready to calm our emotional seas. We need only to walk toward Him on the bridge of prayer.

Scripture for Further Meditation:
Do not be anxious about anything,
but in everything, by prayer and petition,
with thanksgiving, present your requests to
God. And the peace of God, which transcends
all understanding, will guard your hearts
and your minds in Christ Jesus.
Philippians 4:6–7

*Dear Jesus, I thank You for being with me
in the past, for answered prayer, and Your
constant love. In my present confusion,
I cannot see the purpose and I feel lost.
Please give me the faith to trust You now,
knowing Your love and faithfulness will
carry me through and in Your arms I can
know peace once more. Amen.*

Playing Favorites

*Isaac, who had a taste for wild game, loved
Esau, but Rebekah loved Jacob. Genesis 25:28*

Let's face it. Some kids are just easier to love than
others. In years of teaching children of all ages, I've
found there are some who, with little or no effort,
worm their way into my heart. They are agreeable,
eager to please, excited about learning, and teach-
able. Then there are the others. They complain about
everything, act bored, disagree just to be disagree-
able, and think they already know everything. The
second group probably needs more love than the first,
but rarely gets it!

Even within a family, there are those who just seem to get along with others more easily. It's understandable that mothers would prefer to be with the child who is pleasant and cheerful, but as mothers, we can't afford to play favorites. When we do, we breed jealousy and hatred within the walls of our homes. That's what happened to Rebekah.

Her twin sons were not at all alike. Their appearance differed and so did their personalities. Esau was a ruddy and hairy fellow who loved hunting and wandering in the open country. Jacob, pale and smooth-skinned, was a stay-at-home type with a talent for cooking. Perhaps because she spent more time with Jacob, Rebekah favored him. But in choosing one son over the other, she engaged in a dangerous game that almost ended in murder! Playing favorites destroyed the harmony of Isaac and Rebekah's home.

As mothers we should be especially careful to treat each child with equal dignity and love. This doesn't mean we must treat each child exactly the same. I knew a family once where gifts and attention were doled out with excruciating equality. If one got a toy truck, the other got the same truck even if he preferred a car. If one received piano lessons, so did the other, despite the fact that he wanted to play the drums. In their quest to be totally fair, they were ignoring their children's differences. Loving each child equally means taking the time to get to know each one and understanding what is meaningful and valued by each. Sometimes it requires setting aside our own preferences to appreciate the unique personalities of our children.

This kind of love mirrors our Savior's love for us. He doesn't require each of us to behave exactly the same, to have the same personality or appearance. He cherishes our individuality, but expresses His love equally to all. And He can empower us as we strive to do the same with our own children. By refusing to play favorites, we encourage harmony in our homes.

Scripture for Further Meditation:
I charge you, in the sight of God and Christ Jesus and the elect angels, to keep these instructions without partiality, and to do nothing out of favoritism. 1 Timothy 5:21

Prayer:

Dear Father, thank You that You treat all of Your children without favoritism. Help me as I raise my own children to look at each with the eyes of love. May I help them to understand that I do not favor one over the other, but cherish each as a special gift from You. In Jesus' name. Amen.

Do It for Me

*His mother said to him, "My son, let the curse
fall on me. Just do what I say; go and get
them for me." Genesis 27:13*

I heard a young man speak at church the other
day. He was a gifted minister, able to bring the
Scriptures alive through his teaching. When he gave
his testimony, however, he shared how he had spent
years thinking of himself as a failure. His father had
wanted him to be a doctor. From the time he was
small, this dream had guided all his decisions. His
dad didn't want him to play football because he
might injure his hands. In high school he wasn't
allowed to take electives such as speech, drama, or
debate because his dad wanted him to take extra science and math courses instead. His father offered to
pay for his college education, but only if he majored
in pre-med and then went on to medical school. For
years the young man stifled his desire to study philosophy and religion and tried to be what his father
wanted. And for years he was miserable. Then one
day he stood up to his dad and followed his heart.
Eventually he became a pastor and his joy at sharing
the Gospel was undeniable. While his father and he
finally reconciled, he regretted the years of fellowship that were sacrificed at the altar of his dad's
ambition.

As mothers we all have dreams for our children,

but they are *our* dreams. While it is our privilege to guide and encourage our children to explore their options in life, it is not our right to force them to live out our goals. To do so denies the movement of the Holy Spirit within their hearts. God has created each of them with wonderful and unique talents, abilities, and drives. Our task is to help them discover what it is God has gifted them to do. For some mothers this is a frightening prospect. But when we understand that God loves them even more than we do, we can trust Him to lead them where they should go. When we try to influence our children to fulfill our own egos and dreams, we risk diverting them from the path God wants them to take. Because of Rebekah's self-centered maneuvering, Esau and Jacob were estranged and Isaac was betrayed. How much better it would have been to allow God to work out His plan for her family—in His way and time.

When we are tempted to maneuver our children's lives, let's remember the lesson of Rebekah's life. After all, God is able to do a far better job at directing them as they should go—and His ways are unlimited!

Scripture for Further Meditation:
Teach me Your way, O Lord, and I will walk in Your truth; give me an undivided heart, that I may fear Your name. Psalm 86:11

*Dear Jesus, forgive me when I confuse my
desires for my children with Your desires
for them. Help me to encourage them to
prayerfully seek Your direction for their lives
so they might experience the joy of fulfilling
Your will. Amen.*

What a Tangled Web!

*Then Rebekah said to Isaac, "I'm disgusted
with living because of these Hittite women.
If Jacob takes a wife from among the women
of this land, from Hittite women like these, my
life will not be worth living." Genesis 27:46*

By the time Rebekah's plots were completed, she
had changed from comforter to conniver! What happened to the sweet young wife who obediently wed
her beloved bridegroom? It appears that Rebekah's
focus moved from what God would have her do to
what she wanted done. As we saw earlier, this motive
drove her to favor one child over the other, to execute
a devious plan to cheat her elder son, and then it cul-
minated in a dramatic lie to her husband. She bought

into the philosophy that the ends justify the means. And so she sacrificed her integrity to accomplish her goals.

While we may look at Rebekah with a degree of objectivity, I wonder if we are quite so unbiased when examining our own motives. Are there times when I, just like Rebekah, use emotions, half-truths, and deception to get my husband to do what I desire? Have I developed the habit of conniving to get my way and then excusing it as legitimate because the end results seem beneficial? If so, I risk unraveling the very fabric of our love.

Remember the comfort Rebekah provided Isaac when their marriage was new? Recall the tender prayers he offered to God on her behalf? What happened? Just like many of us, it appears that Isaac and Rebekah settled into habits of seeking their own individual desires, instead of continuing to grow as a couple. We do not know if their trust and devotion were ever restored, but if our own marriages are on shaky grounds, we can turn to God and ask Him to help us restore the trust within our own marriages.

God desires for husband and wife to become one (Genesis 2:24). This oneness needs to be maintained, however. Making time for each other, praying with and for each other, listening to each other, putting the other's needs first are all ways to knit our hearts together as husband and wife. If your marriage has lost that initial feeling of closeness, spend time working to rediscover it. Many churches sponsor excellent marriage enrichment classes on weekends. Prayer and fellowship with other Christian couples also can encourage you to find ways to rekindle your love. With God, it is never too late to change and He delights in the task of restoring relationships.

Scripture for Further Meditation:
However, each one of you also must love his wife as he loves himself, and the wife must respect her husband. Ephesians 5:33

Prayer:

Dear Jesus, thank You for my husband. Help me to honor him with respect, truth, and love; to comfort him as You have comforted me. Thank You for our marriage. May it always bring glory to You. Amen.

$\mathcal{R}uth$

A Stranger Who Came Home

I AM RUTH OF MOAB, THE DAUGHTER-IN-LAW OF NAOMI of Bethlehem. I came to Judah as a penniless widow, a stranger and foreigner. But the God of Israel had a plan for my life that was more wonderful than I could imagine.

When my father-in-law, brother-in-law, and husband died, I was without hope. My mother-in-law, Naomi, was determined to return to the land of her birth. She urged me to return to my father's home, where there was a chance for me to remarry and have a family of my own. My sister-in-law, Orpah, decided to obey Naomi's guidance, but something kept me from doing so. It was as if I was bound to this old woman with ties stronger than blood, and I pleaded with her to let me stay with her. I longed to learn more about her people, the Israelites, and her God, Yahweh, and to make their home my own.

We walked for days over dusty roads and along the banks of the river, traversing desolate valleys and navigating wilderness areas before reaching the city of Bethlehem on a hot afternoon in the midst of the barley harvest. Naomi was weak and in distress, without a husband or sons to provide for her. So I traveled to the fields of Boaz where I was allowed to glean the fields behind the harvesters. It was tiring work, but provided us with food, and although I worked long hours, we had plenty of barley to eat. When Boaz returned from town to greet the harvesters, he saw me working and inquired about me. Then, in kindness and generosity, he offered to allow me to remain in his fields and even to sit at his table for meals!

When I shared what I had been given with Naomi, her eyes shone with hope and love. She could see God's hand in the kindness of Boaz. His protection would ensure our security.

The day came, however, when Naomi saw more than the provision of food in the heart of Boaz. She disclosed to me her desire to secure a home for me where I could enjoy the fulfillment of a husband and children. Carefully explaining the customs of her country, she instructed me to present myself to my benefactor and seek his protection as kinsman-redeemer. I was frightened and excited all at once. Could it be that I might indeed rise above the place of a foreigner and outcast? In obedience to Naomi, I followed all her instructions and a plan more wonderful than I could have dreamed was set in motion.

Within a few weeks, Boaz had redeemed me from the claims of another and brought me to his own home as his wife. In time I came to see the hand of God in every step of my life. The things I had thought were lost He restored, and He blessed us with a son we named Obed. All the elders bore testimony that our child would grow strong, and the women of the village prayed that he would be famous throughout Israel. In the Lord's mercy and grace, He took a lonely widow without a country and gave her a home in the family of God. 🌸

Hungry for God

But Ruth replied, "Don't urge me to leave you
or to turn back from you. Where you go I will
go, and where you stay I will stay. Your people
will be my people and your God my God."
Ruth 1:16

Ruth's life to this point had not been easy. She was
a Moabite woman who married a foreign believer in
Yahweh. After several years of marriage, her husband
died and left her a childless widow. Her mother-in-
law, Naomi, decided to pack up and move back home
to Judah where Ruth would be considered an outsider
and unsuitable for marriage. Her past was filled with
sorrow, her present with emptiness, and her future
appeared bleak. But Ruth had hope. She refused to
look at her circumstances and despair, and instead
grasped at the faith she witnessed in Naomi. She was
hungry for God.

When my world is crumbling around me and my
dreams lie in pieces at my feet, for what do I hunger?
Too often I hunger to be pitied, to be carried by
another, to have my questions answered, to have
company in my misery. But none of these things
brings about a permanent solution for my needs.
Only God can provide what I truly need, and it is
only in Him I will find renewed hope and the peace
I seek.

It is easy, when the life we planned isn't working

out, to try to fix things using our own intelligence and ingenuity. When my husband and I had trouble conceiving a child, I spent hours searching through books and articles in the library. I visited several different doctors and talked to other women who had struggled with infertility. I submitted to all kinds of painful medical procedures and exploratory surgeries. Oh, I prayed too, but it was usually on the way to an appointment or the library. I was so busy stuffing myself with information and man-made solutions, I had no hunger to know what God had in mind. Most of all, I just wanted to inform Him how He could cooperate with my plans!

One day, after years of unsuccessful attempts to "do it my way," I sat alone and discouraged. I had run out of ideas. Everywhere I looked I saw closed doors. Not only were my arms empty, but my heart felt empty and I finally began to experience hunger pangs to be closer to God. He led me not to a maternity ward, but to a Bible study where I immersed myself in His Word. Slowly, steadily He began to fill me with His comfort and compassion. Week after week I feasted upon the riches at His table, and I felt myself becoming satisfied. I had a strange new feeling of contentment and assurance that God was in control of my life and would do much better with it than I had. On the very last day of the Bible study, as we completed our year of lessons in Matthew, I received a phone call saying we were to become parents of a precious 7-week-old baby boy! In His mercy and perfect timing, God satisfied all my hunger and filled me to overflowing!

> **Scripture for Further Meditation:**
> *He has filled the hungry with good things,*
> *but has sent the rich away empty.*
> *Luke 1:53*

Prayer:

Dear Father, give me a holy hunger to seek You. Fill the emptiness of my heart with the fullness of Your Word and satisfy my soul with good things from Your hand. Thank You for your everlasting kindness to me, Your child. In Jesus' name. Amen.

Willing Heart, Humble Hands

> *And Ruth, the Moabitess said to Naomi, "Let me go to the fields and pick up the leftover grain behind anyone in whose eyes I find favor." Naomi said to her, "Go ahead, my daughter." Ruth 2:2*

Don't you get tired of doing the same meaningless jobs day after day? At home it's the never-ending cycles of laundry, meal preparation, house cleaning. Outside the home it might be the repetition of a factory job, the constant serving of customers, or the relentless mountain of paperwork. Where's the excitement we once dreamed about? Does anyone care, let alone notice what we do day after day, year after year?

It's easy to be discouraged under these circumstances—especially when we have a "what's in this for me?" attitude. If we observe Ruth, however, I think we can learn a valuable lesson about meaningful work: It involves a willing heart and humble hands.

With God working through her, Ruth recognized the desperate situation she and Naomi faced—no food and no income—and she purposed in her heart to help. She didn't mope or complain or blame Naomi for their circumstances. Nor did she wait to be asked to help. Ruth offered her services willingly. And then she did not shrink from a lowly position. It didn't matter if the job was beneath her skill levels or lacked excitement. With simple and beautiful humility she set out to do it well.

Around the house, in the workplace, at our churches there are jobs that need doing. They may not be exciting, but unless they are accomplished, needs go unmet. We can do the work grudgingly with sour faces and complaints or we can adopt Ruth's attitude of a willing heart and humble hands. When we choose to do our work as a service to others instead of status for ourselves, we participate in a process that brings glory to God and builds His kingdom.

Imagine the difference in our churches if we all worked with willing hearts and humble hands. There would be no more panicked pleas for nursery helpers, vacation Bible school workers, or kitchen volunteers. If our homes were infused with Ruth's attitude, they would echo with harmony, not harangues, and our workplaces would be filled with cooperation instead of conflict. When we put our hearts and hands together for Christ, God can transform our work, wherever we are.

Scripture for Further Meditation:
I have set you an example that you should do as I have done for you. I tell you the truth, no servant is greater than his master, nor is a messenger greater than the one who sent him. Now that you know these things, you will be blessed if you do them. John 13:15–17

# Prayer:

*Father, forgive me when I resent the work
You have given me to do. Help my heart to
be willing and my hands humble as I serve
others and You. May my reward be to see
Your kingdom come on earth as it is in
heaven. Amen.*

Bountiful Blessings

*Boaz replied, "I've been told all about what
you have done for your mother-in-law since
the death of your husband—how you left
your father and mother and your homeland
and came to live with a people you did not
know before. May the LORD repay you for what
you have done. May you be richly rewarded
by the LORD, the God of Israel, under whose
wings you have come to take refuge."
Ruth 2:11–12*

Have you ever felt invisible? Maybe you're the one
who always sits in the back row, who bakes the cookies but never serves them, makes the costumes and
sets but is never onstage. You're a perpetual second

fiddle, playing in the background. Perhaps you don't seek the spotlight and are happy to be supporting others, but aren't there times when you wonder if anyone even knows you exist?

Ruth was just such a woman. She wasn't one of the "in-crowd" gathered around the well every morning, sharing neighborhood gossip and barley cake recipes. She was a foreigner, a heathen, a widow, penniless. No one knew anything about her and no one particularly cared to find out. They let her do her own thing, trailing after the others, gathering up their leftovers. But Ruth didn't seem to be bothered by all this. Why?

We are given a clue in the verses above where Boaz speaks to Ruth. Ruth was not motivated by a need to be noticed—or even appreciated. She did not expect people to make allowances for her just because her life had been difficult. Ruth worked out of love for another. She loved her dear mother-in-law, Naomi. And we know from previous passages, she loved the God Naomi worshiped. Her work was not merely a means to an end, it was also a service motivated by gratitude. Recognizing this, Boaz commended Ruth and offered a beautiful prayer on her behalf, asking God to reward her generosity and diligence with His abundant blessings.

When we labor, whether at home, church, in an office, or at another job, we have the same opportunity as Ruth. We can approach work as an unpleasant drudgery to get through, or as a gift of service to others and to God. If we often feel our work is unrewarding, perhaps it is because our attitudes create a barrier to His blessing. Resentment, complaints, and bitterness are not evidence of a joyful servant experiencing the Lord's rich rewards. If my work is unrewarding, maybe I need to ask God to cultivate in me a heart like Ruth's. For when I can serve others and God where I work, I too will experience His bountiful blessings.

Scripture for Further Meditation:
Whatever you do, work at it with all your heart, as working for the Lord, not for men, since you know that you will receive an inheritance from the Lord as a reward. It is the Lord Christ you are serving.
Colossians 3:23–24

Prayer:

Dear Jesus, thank You that You came to earth to do the work of redemption so I could know the blessings of forgiveness and salvation. As I work, help me to do it with a servant's heart so I may not only receive blessings, but also be a blessing where You have placed me. Amen.

A Generous Spirit

So Ruth gleaned in the field until evening.
Then she threshed the barley she had gathered,
and it amounted to about an ephah. She carried
it back to town, and her mother-in-law saw
how much she had gathered. Ruth also brought
out and gave her what she had left over after
she had eaten enough. Ruth 2:17–18

Ruth was a giver. She gave her time and her strength, toiling from early in the morning until evening in the fields doing the back-breaking work of gleaning, picking up the leftover stalks of barley behind the hired workers. When it was too dark to glean, she spent a couple of hours threshing what she had gathered. She ended up with an ephah or about half a bushel of barley, weighing approximately 30 pounds. This she hoisted in a jar or bag, probably upon her head, and walked back to her home. Arriving at Naomi's humble dwelling, Ruth presented her mother-in-law not only with all the grain she had gleaned, but also the leftovers from her lunch with Boaz. She gave her time, her energy, and now, all her material wealth as well. Ruth had a generosity of spirit that overwhelmed those around her.

I must confess that it is not always easy for me to be generous. I want to hoard portions of my time, my energy, even my material wealth for myself. I set limits upon how much I am willing to give. I hear myself saying things like, "I worked on vacation Bible school for the past five years. Let someone else do it!" "I just gave to the Christmas mission drive and now they want more for the Easter offering!" "I worked all day, let someone else fix dinner for a change!" "I'm tired of always being the one who has to stop what I'm doing to ... (fill in the blanks, mothers!)."

Although I don't like to admit it, at the core of all these kinds of statements lurks the seed of selfishness. I resent giving beyond the limits I have set as reasonable. But when I look at how God worked in Ruth, I see a spirit directed by generosity, not selfishness. She didn't hold back part of the barley as her right since she worked all day gathering it. She refused to keep the tasty leftovers for a midnight snack even though they were hers and Naomi would never know. When you have a generous spirit, you do not count every act, every minute, every dime according to how it will benefit you, but how it can be used to bless others. Like our Savior, Ruth possessed a spirit of generosity. She was a giver, not a taker.

Scripture for Further Meditation:
Remember this: Whoever sows sparingly will also reap sparingly, and whoever sows generously will also reap generously. Each man should give what he has decided in his heart to give, not reluctantly or under compulsion, for God loves a cheerful giver. 2 Corinthians 9:6–7

Prayer:

Dear Father, please forgive the selfishness that so often directs my choices. Help me to remember the generosity with which You lavish Your love upon me, especially in the giving of Your own dear Son for me. May I, in response, develop a spirit of generosity that gives cheerfully of my time, energy, and wealth to others. In Jesus' name. Amen.

An Obedient Heart

"Wash and perfume yourself, and put on your best clothes. Then go down to the threshing floor, but don't let him know you are there until he has finished eating and drinking. When he lies down, note the place where he is lying. Then go and uncover his feet and lie down. He will tell you what to do." "I will do whatever you say," Ruth answered. Ruth 3:3–5

It must have seemed a strange request. Ruth was unfamiliar with the Hebrew culture and I suspect this was not the way things were done where she came from back in Moab. Perhaps she wondered if such a bold yet secretive move would cost her her job in the fields, or bring her ridicule and rejection. But look at her response: "I will do whatever you say." The only motivation for this kind of obedience is love. It is clear that Ruth loved Naomi and love like that produces trust.

In the New Testament, Jesus teaches that love and obedience are two sides of the same coin: "If you love Me, you will obey what I command" (John 14:15). "Whoever has My commands and obeys them, he is the one who loves Me" (John 14:21). Jesus replied, "If anyone loves Me, he will obey My teaching" (John 14:23). It is easy to say that we desire to demonstrate our love for Jesus by living in obedience to Him. But what about the times when He asks us to do things that are uncomfortable or unfamiliar or "just not the way I did things back home!"?

When my children are whining but I'm tired and angry, and words crouch on the tip of my tongue, do I heed Christ's command: "Love one another. As I have loved you, so you must love one another." (John 13:34)? When I am frustrated by the behavior of a coworker and I want to let her have it, do I hear the voice of Jesus saying, "You hypocrite, first take the plank out of your own eye, and then you will see clearly to remove the speck from your brother's eye." (Matthew 7:5)? When my husband is thoughtless or makes a remark that hurts my feelings, do I listen to my Savior's warning, "But if you do not forgive men their sins, your Father will not forgive your sins." (Matthew 6:15)?

Like Naomi's instructions to Ruth, the Lord's commands may not always conform to our personal preferences. Like Ruth, however, we look beyond our own understanding and trust instead upon the love and empowerment of the One guiding us. In the end, Ruth's obedience brought blessing to her family for generations. When we obey the One who in love gave His life for us, our families also are blessed.

Scripture for Further Meditation:
"If you obey My commands, you will remain in My love, just as I have obeyed My Father's commands and remain in His love ...
My command is this: Love each other as I have loved You." John 15:10, 12

Prayer:

Dear Father, forgive me for the times I choose to disobey Your commands and do things my own way. Help me listen to Your Word and to obey it even when it seems difficult. For I know You love me and want to help me become the woman You created me to be. Amen.

A Fruitful Life

So Boaz took Ruth and she became his wife.
And the LORD enabled her to conceive, and
she gave birth to a son ... And they named
him Obed. He was the father of Jesse,
the father of David. Ruth 4:13, 17

Have you ever felt as if your life has no direction?
You get up and go through your routine, doing the
same things day after day. You look back at some
point and wonder what happened to all the dreams
you once cherished. You look ahead and question if
any of your goals will ever be achieved. You can't see
much of the present because there's such a clutter of
demands, needs, and disasters claiming your attention. To paraphrase an old fast food ad: Where's the
fruit?!

I suspect Ruth might have had some of those
same thoughts. She married a fine young man who
had come to live in her country and then he died.
She had no inheritance, no children, no home, and
no prospects. She traveled to a foreign land where
the only person she knew was her bitter, widowed
mother-in-law. Lacking skills and money, she worked
from dawn until dark gathering leftovers in a barley
field. She had no dowry, no hope, no reason to
dream things would ever improve. But Ruth had
something else. Ruth had a hunger to follow God and
a God who could and would fill that hunger with

Himself. With humility and patience, she obeyed His directions one day at a time. Little by little, He revealed His plan for her through the circumstances and relationships of her daily life. He led her from a pagan land into the Promised Land. He released her from the hopelessness of her past and placed her in the lineage of the Messiah. He took the confusion and dreariness of her present and infused it with the brilliance of His love.

Right now, I may not see how God is working in my life. I may even doubt that He cares about the state of my affairs. But my perception is not God's reality. Jesus is at work every day, allowing people and circumstances to impact me so I may have opportunities to live a fruitful life. And what is even more wonderful is that He promises to be with me through every moment of it! Like Ruth, I may encounter hardship, disappointment, and even sorrow. But like Ruth, I can choose to live with patient humility and obedience confident that God, in His good time, will produce good fruit in me.

Scripture for Further Meditation:
"I am the vine; you are the branches.
If a man remains in Me and I in him,
he will bear much fruit; apart from Me
you can do nothing." John 15:5

Prayer:

Dear Jesus, keep me close to You, a healthy branch drawing my strength from the vine of Your love. Let me live with patience and obedience through each season of my life, so that when harvest time comes I may be fruitful. Amen.

Hannah

A Mother of Prayer

I AM HANNAH, WIFE OF ELKANAH OF EPHRATAH. My husband has another wife, Peninnah, who despises me, for although she has given our husband several sons and daughters, he favors me. Even though Elkanah loves me deeply, the emptiness of my womb and Peninnah's constant taunts became more than I could bear. So one year, when we made our annual pilgrimage to Shiloh to worship and sacrifice to the Lord Almighty, I made a decision. I would throw myself upon the mercy of the Lord.

After finishing our meal I rose, and went to the tabernacle. There, in deep anguish, I wept and prayed. If only God would grant my desire for a son,

I vowed that I would relinquish the child back to the Lord for all the days of his life. Eli, the priest who sat by the doorpost of the Lord's tabernacle, at first thought my fervor resulted from too much wine. But after I opened my heart to him, he blessed me and prayed that the God of Israel would grant my request.

My heart lifted in joy, and I had confidence in the power of God on my behalf. Then the Lord remembered me. Within the year I conceived and brought forth my first child, a son I named Samuel, which means *heard of God*. Until he was weaned, Samuel remained in our home, a joy to both his father and me. It would have been easy to keep him there. Yet how could I deny my vow to the Lord when He had granted me the desires of my heart?

The day came when we traveled once again up to Shiloh. But this time we brought little Samuel, for he was to be left in the care of Eli, to be trained as a servant of the Lord. It was not an easy journey, for my heart ached at the thought of leaving my young son in the hands of another. Could I trust Eli to care for my little boy with tenderness and love? But then I remembered the faithfulness of God. I would trust in Him, not in the faithfulness of others.

After leaving Samuel at the temple, the strangest thing happened. Instead of being filled with grief as I had expected, my soul was lifted to new heights of joy! It was as if the Spirit of the Lord flooded my heart and overflowed in a song of praise. A new confidence filled me, and I praised God with words of power and prophecy. It was as if He replaced the emptiness in my soul with Himself, filling me completely.

In the years that followed, I traveled to Shiloh many times, each year carrying a robe I had lovingly made for Samuel. And the Lord continued to bless our family. Samuel grew in grace as he ministered before the Lord under Eli, and Elkanah and I were granted three more sons and two daughters! In all my days I have never seen those who honor the Lord put to shame, and I tell all I know that God is the great Keeper of Promises. ✤

Feeling Empty

[Elkanah] had two wives; one was called
Hannah and the other Peninnah.
Peninnah had children, but Hannah
had none. 1 Samuel 1:2

In Elkanah's household there were the haves and the have-nots. Hannah considered herself a have-not. Oh, she had a lovely home, an adoring husband, beautiful clothes, and servants, but she lacked the one thing that defined her personal worth: children.

For a woman today who longs for a baby, Hannah's emptiness is all too understandable. All the other things in her life fade in importance. She finds it easy to ignore her blessings. She only sees the curse of infertility. I know this first-hand and the memories of disappointment, month after month, year after year are still vivid.

But infertility is not the only thing that can make a woman feel empty. A lack of appreciation, the loss of a loved one, the rebellion of a child, the longing for a career can all cause an emptiness of heart. Like Hannah, we look at others who possess what we desire. Then we examine our own situation and, blinded by their real or perceived fulfillment, we see only how we fall short.

In Hannah's world a woman was measured by her ability to bear healthy children, especially sons. Today a woman may be measured by other standards:

a stunning body, an advanced academic degree, a well-decorated home, a successful career, beautiful and brilliant children. Whatever our society values becomes our plumb line of value and, too often, the determining factor in our self-worth. We compare ourselves to a faulty standard, and we just don't measure up.

If the standards and values of our society are faulty, what is the appropriate measurement of a woman's worth today? It is the same one Hannah should have considered thousands of years ago: It is the gold standard of our inestimable value as a child of God. God's love is not dependent upon what I can produce physically, intellectually, or emotionally. God's love flows from His grace in undeserved abundance. When I learn to focus on Him and His immeasurable love for me, I discover peace, joy, and hope. Jesus fills the empty places in my life!

Scripture for Further Meditation:
May the God of hope fill you with all joy and peace as you trust in Him, so that you may overflow with hope by the power of the Holy Spirit. Romans 15:13

Prayer:

Dear Father, I confess that I sometimes feel empty when I compare myself to others. Help me change my focus and look instead at the blessings I have received from Your loving hand. Fill me with Your Spirit, Lord, until my emptiness is gone. Amen.

Put Down and Piled On

And because the LORD had closed her womb, her rival kept provoking her in order to irritate her. 1 Samuel 1:6

Hannah was not having an easy time of it. God had allowed a trial to enter her life. That was bad enough, but adding insult to injury, she was forced to live with someone whose main aim in life was to make Hannah miserable! Every morning Hannah awoke to the burden of her barrenness, and all day long Peninnah mocked her for it. Life was piling on.

Have you ever felt like that? There's a circumstance in your life you didn't ask for and you can't change. Then, to add to your problems, a relationship falls apart. Hostility and despair team up, and it's a struggle just to get through the day. You wonder if it's all worth it as you stagger under the weight of discouragement.

I suspect Hannah wrestled with the same feelings. She might have been tempted to lash out in anger or sink into depression crying out: "Why me?" "What have I done to deserve this?" "God, have You forgotten me?" When we also struggle with difficulties we didn't cause or people who irritate or provoke us out of jealousy or contempt, how can the Lord help us to respond?

First, it's good to remember that we cannot see all of God's plan from our limited perspective. Yes, God closed Hannah's womb, but at the perfect time He also opened it. Our trial, disability, or loss may be a prelude to a future blessing in God's good time.

Second, we cannot control the behavior of others. We can only control our responses. We do not need to retaliate when others mistreat us. While we ought never to tolerate abuse, through God's working in us, we can be just as intolerant of committing abuse in return. Praying, seeking help, asking the Lord to bless the other person, returning kindness for insult are all options.

Third, we can remember that our circumstances are never a measure of God's care for us. His mercy is always available, His love constant. When we feel put down and piled on, Jesus is there, as near as our heartbeat. He knows what we are going through. For He has been there Himself, and He desires to sustain us with His powerful Spirit. He desires not only to enable us to live in our circumstances, but to rise above them and be blessed by them. He is, after all, the risen Lord.

Scripture for Further Meditation:
O Lord, how many are my foes! How many rise up against me! Many are saying of me, "God will not deliver him." But You are a shield around me, O Lord, You bestow glory on me and lift up my head. Psalm 3:1–3

Prayer:

Prayer: O Lord, sometimes I feel like I can't go on. Thank You that You have provided Jesus so I never have to face anything alone. Help me to count on Your wisdom and courage to live each day as Your beloved child. Amen.

Misunderstood

Elkanah her husband would say to her, "Hannah, why are you weeping? Why don't you eat? Why are you downhearted? Don't I mean more to you than ten sons?" 1 Samuel 1:8

Hannah was blessed with a husband who adored her. He was observant and concerned about both her physical and emotional health. He went out of his way to make her feel special. Yet in all his compassion, he failed to truly understand his wife.

There are times in our lives when the closest friend, the dearest love will not be able to truly understand us. If we are completely honest, we realize even we don't always understand ourselves! We seem to have all we desire, yet we're unhappy. Our lives take a turn for the worse and still we find an inner joy.

Each of us is complex, a mixture of history, experience, genetics, and chemicals blended with emotion and spirit. We are unique creations touched by eternity, living in time. Is it any wonder that we sometimes misunderstand one another? Even with the best intentions, we fall short of fulfilling one another's deepest needs.

During the first 28 years of our marriage, my husband was a naval officer. I have always considered us best friends and soul mates. But God taught me early on that I would never be able to count on my beloved husband to meet all my needs, nor always to be there when I needed understanding. We were married for two weeks when the navy called him away for a month and a half. After nearly a year of marriage, he left for a seven-month overseas deployment that stretched to almost nine months. During his career he missed innumerable birthdays and holidays, the births of two children, and the only major surgery I've had. But God was always present. In sickness and in health, joy and despair, Jesus was not only beside me, He understood what I was going through and had the ability to help me in ways my husband never could.

If we only depend upon others, they will eventually disappoint us. Not because they want to, but because they, like we, are merely human. Only Christ will never fail. Only He will always understand our deepest need. That is why Paul could write to the saints at Philippi: "And the peace of God, which transcends all understanding, will guard your hearts and your minds in Christ Jesus" (Philippians 4:7).

Scripture for Further Meditation:
For we do not have a high priest who is unable to sympathize with our weaknesses, but we have one who has been tempted in every way, just as we are—yet was without sin. Hebrews 4:15

Prayer:

Thank You, Jesus, for always understanding me, even when I may not understand myself. You are a friend who will never forsake me, but will always remain as near as a prayer. Help me to remember that You lived and died so I might know abundant life now and in eternity. Amen.

Crying Out to God

*Once when they had finished eating
and drinking in Shiloh, Hannah stood up.
Now Eli the priest was sitting on a chair by
the doorpost of the LORD's temple. In bitterness
of soul Hannah wept much and prayed
to the LORD. 1 Samuel 1:9–10*

So many times our prayers are carefully crafted. Perhaps we memorized a certain prayer as a child or we made up one of our own that became rote through years of repetition. In a church prayer meeting we may be more concerned about the phrasing and parsing of our prayers than their content. After all, the pastor or our Bible class may be listening. Often we pray what we think others expect us to pray, inserting our automatic responses at appropriate intervals. But that's not how Hannah prayed.

Hannah wasn't thinking about—in fact, didn't care—what anyone else thought. She was talking to God. Elkanah, her husband, may have been mortified at the spectacle she was creating in front of the temple visitors. Peninnah, her rival, probably reveled in Hannah's lack of propriety. No doubt there was snickering in the galleries. Even Eli, the priest, concluded she was drunk! Still Hannah prayed! Oblivious to those around her, she focused only on the One who could do something about her situation. Scripture tells us she "prayed to the LORD."

There have been times in my life when I've felt my prayers got no higher than the ceiling. I spoke the words, but they seemed meaningless. Perhaps I harbored a secret fear that if I truly opened myself to God, He might not approve of what I had to say. Or maybe I just didn't know how to express myself. Whatever the reason, I experienced a disappointing time of prayer. At those times, I have to remember that the God who answers prayer is greater than my disappointment or dissatisfaction with how I prayed—and that even hesitant, frustrating words will be heard by a merciful Father for the sake of Jesus. At other times, I knew God, and I communicated and I ended my prayer time with joy and serenity. These were the times when I literally poured out my heart to God. Sometimes it was in sorrow, sometimes in joy. Like Hannah, however, I forgot the time and place. I didn't care who was listening or what they thought. God and I were having a conversation.

If we desire to experience prayer as something other than a religious duty or ritual, we can take a lesson from Hannah. She was not afraid to stand before her Maker and be totally honest. Her prayer was not prescribed by tradition, but created by her heart. She did not pray so others might approve, but instead cried out to the Lord alone. These are the prayers that touch the throne of God.

Scripture for Further Meditation:
And pray in the Spirit on all occasions with all kinds of prayers and requests. With this in mind, be alert and always keep on praying for all the saints. Ephesians 6:18

Prayer:

Thank You, Lord, for the privilege of prayer. Give me courage to pray without ceasing and in total honesty at all times and in all circumstances. Thank You for Your promise to hear and answer me for the sake of Jesus. Amen.

Believing Behavior

Eli answered, "Go in peace, and may the God of Israel grant you what you have asked of Him." She said, "May your servant find favor in your eyes." Then she went her way and ate something, and her face was no longer downcast. 1 Samuel 1:17–18

Have you ever heard someone quote a Bible verse about trusting God and in the next breath relate how they lie awake nights fretting about their children away at college? Or have you seen someone chewing out her kids after hearing a sermon on patience and self-control? Maybe you've even complained to a friend about your circumstances in the afternoon when your morning devotional topic was about being content! Often our behavior betrays our true beliefs.

It's easy to quote a Bible verse or even give a short talk at the women's meeting encouraging others to take God at His word. But how we act often speaks louder than our words. When people observe our daily lives, do they see a Christian living like Christ, or someone who only talks about Him?

In this passage from 1 Samuel, Hannah has just completed her time of fervent prayer in the temple at Shiloh. The priest, Eli, speaks with her briefly and encourages her to believe that God will answer her request. Note that Hannah's circumstances did not change. A baby did not drop from the sky into her arms. She did not hear the voice of God booming from the temple rafters promising her a son. What changed was Hannah's behavior. And it was her behavior that demonstrated her belief.

First, Hannah went her way. She returned to her everyday situation. She left the place of prayer, willing to return to Elkanah's home where she was subjected to Peninnah's taunts and her own barrenness. She was willing to wait with patience for God's answer.

Second, Hannah ate something. She decided to stop fasting, to quit grieving, to get on with the everyday activities of taking care of herself. She had made her requests known to God, and she knew He had heard her.

Third, Hannah was no longer downcast. She threw off pessimism and put on the mantle of hope. She acted out her faith, which is "being sure of what we hope for and certain of what we do not see" (Hebrews 11:1).

Too many of us say we believe the promises and teachings of Christ, but act as if we do not, betraying our lack of faith by our behavior. Is it any wonder the unbelieving world thinks the church is full of hypocrites? If we are to be women of faith we, like Hannah, must act in faith, daring to behave as we say we believe.

Scripture for Further Meditation:
Do not merely listen to the word, and so deceive yourselves. Do what it says. James 1:22

Prayer:

Forgive me, Father, for the times I have read or heard Your Word and have not acted as if I believed it. Give me the faith to believe You and to live as an example of Christ-like love in my family and in my community. For the sake and in the name of Jesus. Amen.

Declaring God's Faithfulness

*So in the course of time Hannah conceived
and gave birth to a son. She named him
Samuel, saying, "Because I asked the Lord
for him." 1 Samuel 1:20*

I have a friend who has walked with the Lord for
most of her 75 years. During that time she has had
many experiences others might term tragic. She lived
with financial difficulties, suffered serious health
problems, endured a difficult marriage, and lost a
child to AIDS. Whenever I am with her, however, she
only talks about the goodness of the Lord. His praises are constantly on her lips, and her eyes shine with
delight at His blessings. She lives declaring God's
faithfulness.

When Hannah held her son, she saw in him the
fulfillment of God's promises. They were a long time
in coming, yet she maintained her hope and, when at
last Samuel was born, Hannah determined to make
him an object lesson. She gave him a name that
meant he was a response from God in answer to his
mother's prayer. Every time she spoke his name or
called him, she was reminded of God's enduring
faithfulness. And every time she introduced him to
someone else, his name provided an opportunity to
praise God. I suspect she could have attributed his
birth to a fluke of nature, good luck, the full moon, or
happenstance. But she didn't. Hannah never failed to

declare God's faithfulness.

Frequently I pray for things to happen, or not happen, for God to preserve and protect those I love or to sustain us in a time of trial. But when my prayers are answered, how often do I name the ways God has blessed and declare them to others? When someone mentions how "lucky" we were to find a perfect home when we were house hunting, when they praise the way we endured a difficulty, do I immediately correct them? Do I tell them that those and so many other blessings were not the result of us winning some mystical fateful lottery, but the hand of God moving with grace and mercy in response to prayer? It may be because I don't wish them to think me a religious fanatic, but most often it's simple negligence or forgetfulness.

Last spring my daughter and I were living in one state while my husband began a new job in another. In order for our move to our new home to work out smoothly, several events needed to occur in a relatively short span of time. Houses and property needed to be bought and sold, family relocated, school applications accepted. After hearing a challenging sermon on prayer, my daughter and I decided to make a list of all our prayer requests (there were 10 very specific ones) and leave a blank after each to write in the date God answered it. Every day we prayed, excited to see what God would do. We filled in the date of the tenth answer to prayer exactly one week before we moved. When our friends marveled at how beautifully all the details for our relocation worked out, we pulled out our list and declared God's faithfulness! It was a strong lesson for us all to recall every day how great He is.

Scripture for Further Meditation:
*I do not hide Your righteousness in my
heart; I speak of Your faithfulness and
salvation. I do not conceal Your love
and Your truth from the great assembly.
Psalm 40:10*

Prayer:

*I praise You, God, for Your faithfulness
to all Your children and thank You for the
many ways You have answered my prayers.
Give me boldness to speak of You to all
I meet so they may be encouraged
to trust in You as well. Amen.*

Planned Obedience

Hannah did not go. She said to her husband. "After the boy is weaned, I will take him and present him before the LORD, and he will live there always." 1 Samuel 1:22

So many times as mothers we think about doing the right thing. We read books about child rearing and may even take classes that urge us to be self-controlled, consistent, and understanding parents. Yet all the information, suggestions, and good advice amount to nothing if we do not make a commitment to act on them. Some of us have the best intentions yet we fail to follow through. When the time for accountability arrives, we wiggle out.

Hannah made a vow before God when she was childless: If God would fulfill the desire of her heart, a son, she would dedicate that child to God's service in the temple (1 Samuel 1:11). To some this might have seemed like a convenient bargain with the Almighty—tell God what He wants to hear, and He'll give you what you want. Hannah, however, was not a shallow believer who took her faith or her God lightly. And this was no easy vow to keep. Imagine the temptation, once she held her tiny son, looked into his eyes, nursed him at her breast, to just say, "Forget it, God, this vow is too tough to fulfill." But Hannah was a remarkable woman, and she did a very wise thing from the time her son was born.

Hannah planned her obedience.

She did this in two ways. First, she reaffirmed her goal to dedicate Samuel to God. She determined to continue in her choice to be true to her word regardless of the cost to herself. Second, Hannah told someone else so she would have a higher degree of accountability and support. Hannah's planned obedience gives us a powerful model as mothers today.

When we desire to change a behavior pattern—to stop yelling, to be more consistent, to refrain from nagging, to implement new methods of discipline, etc.—the temptation is to give up and go back on our resolution when the going gets tough. When we feel tired or are overwhelmed with responsibility, it's easier to do things the old, familiar way. That's when Hannah's pattern of planned obedience and accountability can be helpful to us.

State the plan for change or implementing a new behavior. Write it down. Give it to the Lord in prayer. Then share that resolution with someone who will hold you accountable. When we have a solid plan to obey God and know others are available to help us maintain our convictions, our chances for success increase. And if our resolution fails, we can have confidence that God forgives our backsliding and sends His Spirit to comfort and empower us.

Hannah's decision was not an easy one and fulfilling her vow to God probably brought her personal pain. But it was the right thing—the obedient thing—

to do. She set her heart to accomplish her promise and God blessed her for it. (See 1 Samuel 2:21.)

Scripture for Further Meditation:
Does the LORD delight in burnt offerings and sacrifices as much as in obeying the voice of the LORD? To obey is better than sacrifice, and to heed is better than the fat of rams.
1 Samuel 15:22

Prayer:

Dear Jesus, thank You for always keeping Your promises to me. Help me in my desire to be obedient to You and to fulfill my promises as well. Forgive me when I fail and empower me to be accountable to You and others. Amen.

Glimpsing God

Then Hannah prayed and said: "My heart rejoices in the LORD; in the LORD my horn is lifted high. My mouth boasts over my enemies, for I delight in your deliverance." 1 Samuel 2:1

The verse quoted above is the beginning of a beautiful prayer of praise offered by Hannah immediately after she left her young son, Samuel, in the care of the priests at Shiloh. It is particularly interesting, for in it there is not one word about Hannah's grief over saying good-bye to Samuel. Nor are their requests for God's care and protection of him. The prayer is pure praise directed to the Sovereign God in worship and adoration. Through it we see the source of Hannah's strength in a most difficult personal situation. Her strength comes from the Lord who has given her an unshakable faith in His holiness, goodness, power, and love. How has this simple woman from the hill country of Ephraim managed to glimpse the God of eternity?

The answer lies in what God allowed Hannah to endure and experience to that point in her life. She constantly endured the provocations of her rival, Peninnah. Although loved by her husband, she was denied the blessing of children. For years her prayers appeared to be unanswered. When she brought her plight to the temple of God, the priest insulted her. When her prayers were finally answered, she fulfilled a costly vow by relinquishing her first-born into the care of a priest whose sons had questionable characters. Throughout this, Hannah chose to believe in the sovereignty of God. She did not look at her circumstances or to other people for affirmation, but only to Him. Day by day, as she walked in faithfulness, her vision of God grew until she glimpsed through Spirit-filled eyes the truth about God and about humankind.

How many of us have longed for a glimpse of God? Religious writers and seminar leaders, TV personalities and preachers all work to help us "find God" in one way or another. While many programs and lessons are valuable, they often offer shortcuts for those of us who think we're too busy to experience God the "old fashioned" way. In truth, however, if we want to really catch a glimpse of God, we need to go where God is found—in His Word and the Lord's Supper. We can ask God to help us, like Hannah, endure our circumstances with grace. As she did, we can take our deep needs to God and offer our broken hearts as a sacrifice. Counting on God to be true to His Word, we are able to give Him the glory for answered prayer and lift Him up in undiluted praise. These things are not easy, but I know my Lord and Savior Jesus will empower my obedience and graciously forgive my failures. Then I can share in that same blessing Hannah experienced: the opportunity to glimpse the living God.

Scripture for Further Meditation:
Blessed are the pure in heart, for they will see God. Matthew 5:8

Prayer:

*Dear heavenly Father, please help me
to live in such a way that I may glimpse
You in every aspect of my life. Through
Your Word, reveal Yourself to me. Help me
to constantly raise my voice in praises to You.
In Jesus' name. Amen.*

When Seeing Isn't Believing

*Then Elkanah went home to Ramah, but
the boy ministered before the LORD under
Eli the priest. Eli's sons were wicked men; they
had no regard for the LORD. 1 Samuel 2:11–12*

I'll never forget the feeling as I stood on the side-walk watching my son go into his kindergarten class-room the first day of school. I felt like I was no longer going to be there to protect and defend him. How would he manage if someone bullied him? Who would help him if he struggled with a problem? How would I deal with the negative influences he was bound to encounter? I experienced those same feel-ings again when he entered junior high and high school, and once more when I kissed him good-bye and watched him walk onto an airplane to fly thousands of miles away to college. As mothers, we are constantly saying good-bye to our children, relinquishing them to the influence of others.

When Hannah took little Samuel, who was probably 3 or 4 years old, to live under the authority of the priests at the temple, she undoubtedly hoped he would be cherished and tenderly cared for. In reality, the temple did not seem a friendly place for a little one. Eli was busy and distant, and his sons, the Scriptures say, were wicked. Again Hannah needed to trust a God she could not see. As a woman of prayer, she likely brought her son daily before the throne of the Almighty, asking for His protection and mercy to surround Samuel since her arms no longer could. If she looked at the circumstances, it would be easy to become discouraged. But looking to God brought hope and encouragement.

When my family members are in situations where I cannot see solutions, when they endure difficulties over which I have no control, I can be like Hannah. Although I have no power to change circumstances, I do have the power of God available through Word and Sacrament. I can also daily bring my children before His throne and seek His guidance, protection, grace, and mercy for them wherever they are. This is one of the sacred privileges of motherhood. And the assurance we have is that the same God who guided Samuel and comforted Hannah is available to guide our children and comfort us. He knows and loves our sons and daughters even more than we do and is able to accomplish great things in their lives—things beyond our limited sight that He has prepared for them to do for Him and His kingdom.

Scripture for Further Meditation:
We live by faith, not by sight. 2 Corinthians 5:7

Prayer:

Dear Jesus, sometimes I look at the circumstances around me and I'm afraid for my children. Increase my trust in You so I might daily give them into Your care. Strengthen me to believe that Your loving power and provision is stronger than my limited sight. Amen.

Blessing Our Children

Each year his mother made him a little robe and took it to him when she went up with her husband to offer the annual sacrifice. 1 Samuel 2:19

I can picture Hannah at home, spinning thread from the wool of the sheep or perhaps twisting flax into fibrous strands. Then she would dye the threads and painstakingly weave them into cloth from which to make a special robe to take to Samuel each year on the anniversary of his dedication to the Lord's service. The process was lengthy, but no doubt a sweet labor of love. I imagine Samuel's joy as Hannah hugged him and placed the robe on his growing body and the memory of her embrace as he wore this special garment throughout the year. What a blessing it must have been for Samuel!

Whether our children are still at home, away at college, or grown and living far from us, we can offer them the blessing of a gift of love. These gifts need not be extravagant, for their value lies not in their price tag, but in the love they represent. A note in a lunch bag, a surprise tucked in a suitcase, a favorite dinner, a box of cookies, a special book, or some other present chosen with a particular child in mind says, "I love you and am praying for you." It's such a simple thing, yet these little reminders of a mother's love build strong bonds of affection and trust. When we take the time to show that we know what is important to each child, we confirm his or her worth.

It's amazing to me what a profound impact these gestures of love can have. Last fall I made a huge batch of gingerbread cookies shaped like pumpkins, frosted them with brilliant orange and green frosting, and packed up boxes for one son at college and another who was working and living alone in an apartment. When I spoke with the boys after they had received the cookies, I was surprised to hear each relate the same story. They were rationing themselves to just a couple of cookies each day to make them last as long as possible and each one said how it was like having a little bit of home where they were. A few cups of flour, shortening, sugar, and spice became blessings because they were created and given with love. As mothers we have an opportunity to offer small blessings to our children. Like Hannah we can show them our love and care in a variety of creative ways.

Scripture for Further Meditation:
And if anyone gives a cup of cold water to one of these little ones because he is My disciple, I tell you the truth, he will certainly not lose his reward. Matthew 10:42

Prayer:

Father, I thank You for all the blessings You have poured into my life. Please show me ways I can pass along these blessings to my children in actions and words that remind them of my love for them as well as Yours. In Jesus' name. Amen.

Mothers
from the
New Testament

Elizabeth

Prepared for God's Promises

I AM ELIZABETH, WIFE OF ZECHARIAH, THE PRIEST. My name means "God her oath" and surely God did make and keep an amazing oath to me. At the time when my husband was in the temple performing his priestly duties, the Lord began to do a work of wonder in my life.

As Zechariah stood alone before the altar of the Lord offering incense, a strange thing happened. Gabriel, an angel of the Lord, appeared saying that I would bear a son whom we would call John. This little boy would grow to become a man dedicated to serve God as a prophet in the spirit and power of Elijah. Through him God would turn the hearts of many from wickedness to righteousness. Our son would prepare the way for the Messiah, the long-awaited Redeemer of Israel. When my dear husband heard this proclamation from the angel's mouth, he was amazed and wondered how it could be since we were old and had never experienced the blessing of children. Gabriel spoke again, telling Zechariah that because he doubted the power and word of the Lord, he would be unable to utter one word until the prophecy was fulfilled.

You can imagine my amazement when my husband returned from the temple and related to me in signs and writing what had happened. Together we prayed for God's wisdom and direction. His answer came in a few months as I realized I was with child. I remained in my home, unwilling to share this precious mystery with others, and instead spent my time in contemplation, prayer, and joyful preparation for the coming of our little son. As I waited, a wonder even greater than my own was revealed.

In the sixth month, as I sat one day in the sunshine, a young woman approached our home. As she drew nearer, I recognized her as Mary, my young cousin from Nazareth. I opened my arms to welcome her when a strange thing happened. As Mary spoke her greeting to me, the baby in my womb leapt, and I was filled with such an awareness of God that I began to speak words I had not even contemplated. I praised the Lord for what He had accomplished in

Mary and blessed her for her faith to believe all He had spoken. Then Mary raised her eyes to heaven singing a magnificent prayer of praise to the Lord. Here we were, both mothers-to-be, one young, one old, blessed by God as His chosen vessels.

Dear Mary stayed with me for three months before returning home to walk the path God had prepared for her. And in those weeks we spoke of many things, encouraging and uplifting each other. We could share our deepest thoughts, for each knew the other would understand.

When the time came for our son to be born, he came into the world robust and healthy—and with a cry that announced his birth as loudly as his preaching would one day announce the coming of the Messiah! Eight days later, as we prepared for the circumcision of our baby, the rabbi suggested we name him after my husband. But recalling what Gabriel had said, I cried out, "No! He is to be called John." There was much arguing among those present because there had never been a John in our family. Finally, using signs, they appealed to Zechariah to overrule my choice, but he motioned for a writing tablet and, in firm strokes wrote, "His name is John." As soon as he had written those four words, my husband's voice returned, and the gathered neighbors stood in awe as he spoke forth a prophecy directly from the Lord. In bold words he told of God's plan for John. It was a day of wonder.

As John grew, he matured in heart and soul, always hungry to know more about Yahweh. When he was older, God called him away from home to dwell in the deserts of Judea until the time for his mission arrived. There were times when I did not feel I understood my son, but those were the times when I took comfort in knowing the One who was in control of all our lives. I rejoiced that the God of the promised One had indeed kept His vow to me, His daughter Elizabeth. 🌸

The Right Stuff

His wife Elizabeth was also a descendant of Aaron. Both of them were upright in the sight of God, observing all the Lord's commandments and regulations blamelessly. But they had no children, because Elizabeth was barren; and they were both well along in years. Luke 1:5b–7

If ever there was a woman who deserved a break, according to the world's standards, it was Elizabeth. She came from the right family, had the right husband, lived the right kind of life. In short, she had all the "right stuff." Yet Elizabeth was barren. In her day, that was perceived as a curse from God. I suspect there might have been speculation among the good citizens of the hill country of Judea as to the cause of this "curse." Perhaps they whispered as they drew water, wondering what secret sin Elizabeth kept so well hidden. Maybe the priest's wife wasn't as righteous as she appeared to be! I wonder if even Elizabeth questioned her fate. After all, wasn't she doing all the things God required of her? And if so, wasn't God obliged to bless her?

These kinds of questions and doubts are not exclusive to ancient Judeans. Today we also tend to judge the righteousness of others and the qualification for blessing according to worldly standards. When the devout pastor's wife is stricken with cancer, when the honest businessman is fired, when the hard-working

Christian family suffers one setback after another, we wonder why. After all, aren't these people doing all the "right stuff"? They keep themselves morally pure, they live by biblical standards, they serve the Lord, and are good neighbors. Shouldn't they receive a bonus of blessings or at least some kind of heavenly exemption from trials?

This type of reasoning reflects a faith more suitable to an investment banker than a child of God. It assumes that if you sock away enough good deeds, prayer time, church attendance, and tithes, when your spiritual certificate of deposit comes due, God has to pay up, with interest! And if our investment doesn't return as we expect, we wonder what's wrong with our heavenly CEO!

A study of Scripture should quickly dispel any ideas that the "right stuff" automatically entitles one to material blessings—or even to eternal life. Prophets, priests, and kings, men and women, lived lives of devotion to God, but suffered many trials and tribulations. They realized that their investments were being made in heavenly places and their rewards would be eternal. Their eternal life, they knew, was a gift of God, exclusively from His mercy and grace, not earned by their labor or sacrifices, but by the blood of Jesus. When we allow ourselves to become discouraged because of our circumstances here, we can remember that knowing the Right One is far more important than having the "right stuff."

Scripture for Further Meditation:
But store up for yourselves treasures in heaven,
where moth and rust do not destroy, and where
thieves do not break in and steal. For where
your treasure is, there your heart will be also.
Matthew 6:20–21

Prayer:

Dear Jesus, help me to keep my eyes on You
and not on the world. Help me to rest in the
knowledge that You are working out Your
eternal plan for me according to
Your abiding love. Amen.

Perfect Timing

After this his wife Elizabeth became pregnant
and for five months remained in seclusion.
"The Lord has done this for me," she said.
"In these days He has shown His favor and
taken away my disgrace among the people."
Luke 1:24–25

When Elizabeth's husband, Zechariah, returned
home after his annual two-week stint of duty at the

temple, something amazing happened. Elizabeth became pregnant! This might not have been unusual except for the fact that both Elizabeth and Zechariah were "well along in years," and they had never had a child. If we look back at the angel's announcement to Zechariah in verse 12, we see that the pregnancy is an answer to the priest's prayer. But I wonder when the prayer was made! It is probable that both Zechariah and Elizabeth had prayed often for children when they were young and first married, thinking that was the time God would desire them to raise a family. But as is so often the case, God's timing is not ours.

When we pray and we do not see the answers, we tend to believe God has denied our requests. We sometimes wonder if He even heard them, if He cares, if He answers prayers at all. It is easy to become discouraged if we believe God's timing is the same as ours. But Scripture reminds us that is not the case: "But do not forget this one thing, dear friends: With the Lord a day is like a thousand years, and a thousand years are like a day" (2 Peter 3:8).

One day when my daughter was very young, she brought me a flower she had picked in the garden. It was early spring, and she was anxious to see the daffodils we had planted months earlier. After plucking the long stem, she carefully pried open the bud to find the flower inside and what she handed me was a green stalk with tatters of yellow at the top. It didn't even resemble the beautiful King Alfred bloom pictured on the bulb package. As I carefully explained to her how we had to wait for God to make the bud open, I realized the beautiful lesson He was teaching me through my child. Sometimes, after I plant the bulb of prayer, I am unwilling to wait for God's timing. I try to hurry along the growth process or even force the answer to "bloom" when I think it should. The results are often as disappointing as the tattered daffodil. If I will pray and leave the timing and the way of the answer to the Lord, He will bring it to flower at the perfect time in the perfect way.

Elizabeth realized God's answer to her prayer for a son not when she thought it best, but when her heavenly Father knew it was best. His timing is always perfect.

Scripture for Further Meditation:
But I trust in You, O LORD; I say, "You are my God." My times are in Your hands.
Psalm 31:14–15a

*P*rayer:
Dear Jesus, I thank You that You always hear and answer prayer. Help me to rest in the knowledge that in Your perfect timing, You will bring to flower the plans You have for me. Amen.

Filled to Spill

When Elizabeth heard Mary's greeting, the baby leaped in her womb, and Elizabeth was filled with the Holy Spirit. In a loud voice she exclaimed: "Blessed are you among women, and blessed is the child you will bear!" Luke 1:41–42

Have you ever noticed how people who are filled with God's Spirit seem to overflow with joy? They are constantly encouraging others, looking for ways to improve situations, lifting up those who fall, and giving praise to the Lord for His blessings. It's hard to be around these people and stay in a sour mood! Something about their enthusiasm and positive attitude is contagious.

When the Holy Spirit flooded Elizabeth, she burst forth in praise too. We read in previous verses that she had remained in seclusion for five months after becoming pregnant. Then, in the sixth month, her cousin, Mary, arrived. God caused Elizabeth's unborn child to leap in her womb and, filled with the Spirit, she uttered her beautiful response, confirming to the virgin mother the miracle God had set in motion. How it must have encouraged young Mary to hear these words.

We hear much today about people seeking the Spirit of God. But at times the search appears to be somewhat self-centered. A businessman seeks to be filled with the Spirit so he may make prudent and profitable decisions. A young woman wants the Spirit to fill her so she can discern which young man she should choose as her husband. A graduate student desires the Spirit's filling in order to choose the best career path. While the Holy Spirit *is* a guide and teacher, He is *not* our servant, given to do our bidding.

In fact, if we look at passages describing the third person of the Trinity, it is interesting to note how often the image of water is used. Streams, rivers, fountains, and rain are used at different times to represent the Spirit of God. All these images help us understand the dynamic and life-sustaining nature of the Holy Spirit. As the Father and Son send the Spirit to fill us, we become empowered to spill over with God's love and blessing to others. We can speak words of encouragement, healing, and restoration. We have Christ's strength to endure hardship, offer forgiveness, and live with humility and contentment. We can share in the joy Elizabeth knew as she experienced the presence of God. Through the means of God's Word and the Lord's Supper, the Spirit fills wives and mothers to spill over with God's Spirit; to become rivers of blessings to our families.

Scripture for Further Meditation:
"Whoever believes in Me, as the Scripture has said, streams of living water will flow from within him." By this He meant the Spirit, whom those who believed in Him were later to receive.
John 7:38–39a

 *Prayer:*

Dear Jesus, please cleanse me from my selfish desires and fill me with Your Spirit so I may be a river of living water, flooding my family and neighbors with Your love. Amen.

No Room for Envy

"But why am I so favored, that the mother of my Lord should come to me?" Luke 1:43

I was working on preparations for vacation Bible school at the military chapel where we attended. When I approached one woman about helping in the craft department, she informed me she would only work in the craft department if she could be the chairperson. "After all, I worked as an assistant last year and I think this year I should be able to move up to a role of leadership. I can do just as good a job as Laura, and she has already had a chance to be the chairperson once." When I informed her that Laura would again be leading up the department, she declined to participate. It was clear her motives for service were generated by a need to feel important—to receive top billing.

How different is the attitude of Elizabeth! If you think about it from a purely human perspective, she would have had good reason to be jealous of Mary. After all, Elizabeth was married; Mary was only betrothed. Elizabeth was from a priestly family; Mary was a simple peasant. Elizabeth was mature in years; Mary was a mere teenager. Elizabeth's husband served in the temple; Mary's husband-to-be was a humble carpenter. Elizabeth's son would only be the messenger; Mary's son would be the Messiah! If Elizabeth had been a woman of less character, she might have envied the blessing God bestowed on Mary. But Elizabeth, moved by the Holy Spirit, yielded to God, content to be and do whatever He asked of her, secure in the knowledge that His will was best.

What a powerful example that is for us as wives and mothers today. It is easy to compare ourselves with others and wonder what it would be like to have their talents, blessings, wealth, or relationships. The problem with comparison is that its companion is most frequently envy. Soon our wondering becomes an "if only." If only I had her talent, then I could serve the Lord. If only I had her children, then I wouldn't be so exhausted all the time. If only I had a marriage like hers, then I would be fulfilled. These envious thoughts only lead us to discouragement and discontent.

Instead, we can choose to model our attitudes after Elizabeth. She trusted God and walked the path

He had created for her. Content to serve God in obedience, she was free from jealousy and could honestly rejoice in the way God was blessing her younger cousin. She could encourage Mary with words of love and praise. We can ask God to fill us with the Spirit and to walk with us; He can make us satisfied with the blessings He has given us. We can be secure in the knowledge that He has chosen the very best for each of us.

Scripture for Further Meditation:
*Love is patient, love is kind. It does
not envy, it does not boast, it is not proud.
1 Corinthians 13:4*

Prayer:

*Father, I thank You for the unique gifts
and opportunities You have given to me.
Help me to use all I have to be of service
in Your kingdom and keep me from the sin
of envy. In Jesus' name. Amen.*

Blessings from Belief

"Blessed is she who has believed that what the Lord has said to her will be accomplished!"
Luke 1:45

"It's all well and good for the pastor to tell us to have faith," my friend Anna said. "But I just can't believe God can bring blessings out of this situation."

Anna and her husband were in the midst of a family crisis. Their 16-year-old daughter was pregnant, and they were trying to help her as she struggled to make decisions that would impact all of them deeply.

I could only imagine the anxiety my friend was experiencing, and I wished there were something I could say to encourage her—something that didn't sound like a religious platitude.

It is difficult to imagine blessings resulting from many of the trials we face. When a company downsizes and we're suddenly out of a job, when a loved one becomes seriously ill, when an accident claims the life of a friend, how can we "look for the silver lining"?

Elizabeth's remark to Mary gives us a helpful clue to this mystery. The first thing she notes is that Mary has believed. Now that's interesting. How could Elizabeth know that Mary already believed? Because Mary had just walked several miles to verify what the angel had told her about Elizabeth's unexpected pregnancy. Mary's behavior demonstrated her belief. The second half of Elizabeth's remark indicates that Mary's faith rests not in what she sees, but in the One in whom she believes—what the Lord has said. The third point Elizabeth makes is that Mary's faith does not depend upon the present situation, but upon God's ultimate fulfillment of His promise—upon what will be accomplished.

As I spent time with my friend over the next several months, I was able to share some of the things I learned from Elizabeth. Even when we cannot, in our difficult circumstances, see the reason for believing, we can still cling to the promises of God. We can behave in a way that demonstrates our belief, not in our own abilities to solve our problems, but in God's Word to remain true despite our problems. And in the end we are blessed as we trust Him to accomplish what He has said. He has promised to work all things together for our good because we have been called according to His purpose. When I live believing that, I partake of the blessings Elizabeth shared with Mary two millennia ago.

Scripture for Further Meditation:
And we know that in all things God works for the good of those who love Him, who have been called according to His purpose. Romans 8:28

Prayer:

*Father, when I am in the midst of problems
that threaten to overwhelm me, strengthen
my faith. I believe in Your Word and Your
power to bring peace out of chaos, unity from
division, and hope from despair. Help me
to live in a way that demonstrates this belief.
Amen.*

Breaking the Mold

*On the eighth day they came to circumcise
the child, and they were going to name him
after his father Zechariah, but his mother
spoke up and said, "No! He is to be called John."
Luke 1:59–60*

To us, Elizabeth's announcement that her tiny son
was to be named John doesn't seem very startling.
But in the context of her world, it was quite unusual.
Normally, a son was named for his father or at least
a close male relative. A child's name was part of his
identity and too serious a detail to be left to a mother. So when Elizabeth interrupted the circumcision
ceremony, she was defying convention. She risked

chastisement from the religious establishment and ridicule from her community. But Elizabeth had received a word from the Lord and that was more important than what other people thought.

There are times when we also receive direction or teaching from God that may require us to do or say something out of the ordinary. At such times it is easy to be fearful of what others may think. Being a Christian, however, sometimes means breaking the mold. When everyone in a school PTA meeting seemed to be in favor of a new curriculum that had a clear anti-morals bias, it took courage for a friend of mine to stand alone and speak up against it. When the teens from our church decided to hold a prayer vigil around the flagpole at their high school, it took conviction to silently stand and pray while some of their peers mocked and taunted them. Whenever we speak up for Christian values in a secular society, we take a risk that others may misunderstand, disagree with, criticize, or ridicule us as narrow-minded or intolerant.

Even within our families, our faith may require us to stand alone. The wife who chooses to work toward reconciliation in a difficult marriage, the mother who refuses to cave in to pressure from her teens to do "what everyone else is doing," the sister who declines to support an irresponsible sibling may all find themselves on the outside of the family circle at times. It is not always easy to do the unconventional thing.

But when God is directing us, we can rest assured that we are never really standing alone.

All through Scripture we find examples of men and women who broke the mold of their societies and families. They stood for truth and righteousness when others refused to take a stand. They chose to walk the narrow way when the multitudes ran to the wide and well-trod road. Their society called them misfits, but our Lord calls them heroes.

Scripture for Further Meditation:
Blessed are you when people insult you, persecute you and falsely say all kinds of evil against you because of Me. Rejoice and be glad, because great is your reward in heaven, for in the same way they persecuted the prophets who were before you. Matthew 5:11–12

Prayer:

Dear Jesus, I thank You that You were willing to break the mold and come to earth to provide for my salvation. Help me to be willing to live according to the teachings of Your Word even if it means I must sometimes stand with only You beside me. Amen.

Preparing the Way

And the child grew and became strong
in spirit; and he lived in the desert until
he appeared publicly to Israel. Luke 1:80

Before John was even conceived, the angel Gabriel told Zechariah what his son would become. (See Luke 1:13–17.) When John was only 8 days old, his father, filled with the Spirit, prophesied regarding his son's destiny. (See Luke 1:67–79.) But Zechariah and Elizabeth still had the task of raising their son in such a way that when God called him into service, he would be willing to go. John, like every human child, had a free will.

As mothers we sometimes believe we can make our children turn out a certain way. If we teach and train and work toward the goal of Christian commitment with diligence, won't our kids turn out well? After all, that's what God wants, isn't it? God desires us to raise our children in His nurture and admonition, and He certainly wants each person to grow in his or her personal relationship with Jesus Christ as Savior and Friend. But children aren't like cookies. We can't just put in all the correct ingredients, pop them in the oven for 18 years, and have them come out as spiritually mature believers! What's a mother to do?!

I think we can take some pointers from Zechariah and Elizabeth. We don't know exactly what went on in their home as John was growing up, but we can make some educated assumptions. Being devoted and upright (Luke 1:6) they no doubt raised John in accordance with the Scriptures and regularly participated in worship. Having experienced a personal revelation from God (Luke 1:13–17), they certainly shared their testimony with their young son. As people of prayer (Luke 1:13) they undoubtedly prayed with and for John throughout his life. Having received God's blessings (Luke 1:58), they lived lives of praise and gratitude. In short, they did all they could to provide a home where God was honored in word and actions. With loving devotion they would have prepared John's heart to be ready for God's call when it came to him.

This is the task of each parent today. We can bring our children to the Lord who creates faith in their hearts. As we live our own faith with integrity and commitment daily, we have the opportunity to give our children such an example of the love of Jesus Christ that they grow in their own love for Him. In addition, we have the obligation to instruct them in the Scriptures, bring them to worship, and commit them, body and soul, to the Lord.

Scripture for Further Meditation:
Fathers, do not exasperate your children;
instead, bring them up in the training
and instruction of the Lord. Ephesians 6:4

I have been reminded of your sincere faith,
which first lived in your grandmother
Lois and in your mother Eunice and,
I am persuaded, now lives in you also.
2 Timothy 1:5

Prayer:

Dear Jesus, fill me with Your love so my
children see You in me. Forgive me when
I fail as a parent and guide and direct my
ways and the way of the children You have
entrusted to me. In Your precious name.
Amen.

Mary

The Lord's Servant

I AM MARY, OF THE TRIBE OF JUDAH, of the lineage of David. Born in Nazareth, I grew up in a simple home. We were rich in only one thing—the heritage of faith in Yahweh, the one true God. Although I was young and only a woman, God chose me for the unique and wonderful task of being the mother of Jesus, His only begotten Son.

I had no idea what was happening when the angel appeared and announced that I was favored by the Lord and would bear His Son. How could it be? But as I listened, the Spirit of God opened my heart to understand and to accept the impossible as a possibility. I was willing to be the Lord's servant.

As soon as the angel departed, I hastened to visit my older cousin, Elizabeth, for the heavenly messenger had revealed that she was to bear a child and was already in her sixth month! I longed to speak with her for I loved her and knew her to be a good and godly woman. Arriving at her house, I found things just as the angel had said. Elizabeth confirmed the heavenly proclamation and God filled my mouth with songs of praise. For three months we prayed and encouraged each other and then it was time for me to return home.

Joseph, my betrothed, doubted the truth when I explained the circumstances of my pregnancy, and I could not blame him. Hadn't I been incredulous myself? As I recalled the angel's claim that "nothing is impossible with God," I prayed for the Lord to open Joseph's eyes. And in His grace, God provided an angel to Joseph, speaking to him of the child I would bear and even revealing His name—Jesus, which means "the Lord saves."

There are those who believe that if the Lord chooses you, your life will be trouble-free and prosperous. The truth is different, but even more wonderful. I have learned that when the Lord chooses one for service, life often becomes difficult and more complicated, but God is as close as a heartbeat, providing the riches of His love and fellowship every moment of the day. So it was with Joseph and me. Jesus was born in a rude stable, wrapped in humble swaddling cloths, and laid in a feeding trough. Although He was King, He was attended only by sleepy animals and simple shepherds. When we presented Him at the temple, we could only afford two doves as an offering. Mysterious foreigners brought Jesus priceless gifts, but our countrymen ignored him and within two years of His birth, the ruler of Jerusalem vowed to murder Him. Yet through all these circumstances the Lord protected us, providing wisdom and strength.

When we returned to our hometown, life was simple and ordinary for many years. Jesus was an obedient child, growing in wisdom and stature, and in favor with God and men. Often little things would happen to remind me that He was not my child but God's, and I would save up these memories, treasuring them in my heart. I knew the time would come when He would leave me to accomplish the task for which He was born. I knew it, but my mother's heart feared what it would mean.

The day came when Jesus embraced me and declared that He must be about His Father's business. He left our tiny village of Nazareth and set out on the path prepared for Him from the foundation of the earth. For three years He walked throughout the countryside, healing, raising the dead, miraculously feeding multitudes, teaching us all what it meant to belong to the kingdom of God. Many followed, but few truly believed and I ached for Him, knowing that His heart would be broken by those He came to love.

In the end, they placed Him on a cross outside the city gates, and I stood and wept as I watched Him suffer there. They pierced the hands I had kissed and the feet I had taught to walk. But they could not take His life from Him. That He freely gave.

Although they believed they had vanquished Him, their proud boasts were empty—as empty as the tomb where they tried to keep Him. And those of us who knew and trusted Him witnessed His victory as He ascended to the Father. I raised my eyes and watched the clouds of heaven enfold my son knowing I would live with Him forever. And in my heart I heard the echo of the angel's words: "For nothing is impossible with God!" 🌿

Thy Will Be Done

"How will this be," Mary asked the angel, "since I am a virgin?" "For nothing is impossible with God." "I am the Lord's servant," Mary answered. "May it be to me as you have said." Then the angel left her. Luke 1:34, 37–38

Whenever the story of Jesus' birth is retold, I am awed by Mary's response to the angel's announcement. I think her attitude about her immediate future is a miracle in itself! What faith this young woman had to accept the unbelievable circumstances just described by Gabriel and calmly respond, "May it be to me as you have said." In other words: "Thy will be done."

Few of us will ever encounter angel messengers and none of us will experience the same situation as Mary. But still, as mothers, we face things we consider impossibilities. And for those times there are some comforting lessons in this conversation between Mary and Gabriel.

First is the understanding that we are always free to ask God questions when we do not understand what is happening. It is okay to express our doubts and fears and confusion to Him. I know some Christians who believe that even to hint that you wonder about something God is doing reflects a lack of faith. That's not the example we have in Scripture. The prophets, kings, and apostles all questioned God.

And He often answered their honest questions with loving explanations. Sometimes He was silent, but He never punished them for asking.

Second we learn the unequivocal truth that "nothing is impossible with God." Are you faced with relationships that are broken and wonder if they can ever be mended? Is there a health crisis in your family and you can't see any hope? Are you in the midst of a financial disaster? Have you watched your dreams fade one by one? Does it seem that you're in an emotional pit with no way of escape? Remember the angel's words: "Nothing is impossible with God."

Third is the lesson of Mary's willingness to cast her life into God's hands without reservation. What better place could there be when we stand before a great challenge? As a mother I know there will always be times when I cannot understand what God's purposes are. That is when I want to recall Mary and live by her example: Prayerfully seek understanding, trust in God to do the impossible, and submit my will to His.

Scripture for Further Meditation:
"This, then, is how you should pray:
'Our Father in heaven, hallowed be Your
name, Your kingdom come, Your will be done
on earth as it is in heaven.' " Matthew 6:9–10

Prayer:

Dear Father, please strengthen me when I face things that seem impossible. Help me remember that Your power and love are unlimited and that Your desire is for me to submit my will to Yours. In Jesus' name I pray. Amen.

A Singing Heart

And Mary said: "My soul glorifies the Lord and my spirit rejoices in God my Savior, for He has been mindful of the humble state of His servant." Luke 1:46–48

Have you ever had one of those days when you just can't stop singing? The melodies echo through your mind, and you find yourself humming as you do the laundry, or whistling while you walk the dog, or singing in the shower. There's something about joy that refuses to be contained!

It spills over into our actions and attitudes too. When we're filled with joy it's easy to let up on the gas pedal and let the other guy merge into our lane. We don't get perturbed when little things go awry or we have to wait because the cashier makes a mistake. It's easier to forgive, to look on the bright side, to encourage others, and to let offenses go. Joy transforms us.

When the reality of God's miracle sinks into Mary's heart, she too is transformed by joy. Her soul and spirit burst forth in a beautiful song of praise. The music of heaven echoes in her words, and thousands of years later we still hear and repeat her refrain.

If God is unchanging and His blessings never-ending, why is it that so many of us have forgotten how to sing songs of joy? Is it because we have become so consumed by the cares of our earthly lives that we neglect our spiritual life? When we spend more time reading newspapers and magazines than we do reading the Bible, when we spend more time on the phone than we do in prayer, it's no wonder we sense our joy draining away. It is the contemplation of God's nature and blessings that renews our joy. When we take no time for such contemplation, we risk losing our joy.

I visited a friend recently and saw a plaque on her wall. It pictured a frazzled-looking woman and said: I'm too busy not to pray! Funny, but all too true! It is when we are under the most pressure, facing difficult circumstances, that we are to take time to commune with God. As He reminds us in His Word of His peace in the midst of our distress, His abundance in the midst of our emptiness, His provision in the midst of our need, our hearts, like Mary's, are filled to overflowing with praise and thanksgiving. As Jesus floods us with His love, we too sing for joy, rejoicing in God, our Savior.

Scripture for Further Meditation:
Sing to the LORD a new song; sing to the LORD, all the earth. Sing to the LORD, praise His name; proclaim His salvation day after day. Declare His glory among the nations, His marvelous deeds among all peoples. Psalm 96:1–3

Prayer:

Dear Lord, I thank You for Your gift of salvation and for sustaining me day after day. May my joy in You overflow in songs of praise all the days of my life. Amen.

Misunderstandings

This is how the birth of Jesus Christ
came about. His mother Mary was pledged
to be married to Joseph, but before they came
together, she was found to be with child through
the Holy Spirit. Because Joseph her husband
was a righteous man and did not want to
expose her to public disgrace, he had
in mind to divorce her quietly.
Matthew 1:18–19

Sometimes people just don't understand. Even people who love and care for you may not see your situation with clarity. Just look at Mary's predicament. She was betrothed to Joseph. In those days the betrothal period lasted one year during which time the couple was known as husband and wife although they did not live together and abstained from sexual union. A betrothal was so binding that the breaking of it required a decree of divorce. Then Mary had to reveal to Joseph that she was pregnant. We don't know if she told him about the angel's announcement or not, but we may assume from his decision to divorce her that Joseph believed she had been unfaithful to him. I suspect there was also a lot of whispering around the well in Nazareth as to the paternity of Mary's child. And if she had publicly defended herself with the true story of her baby's conception, do you suppose the neighbors would have believed it? Mary was blessed by God, filled with the Holy Spirit, carrying the Messiah in her womb, yet misunderstood by those she loved.

There are times when we may feel a bit like this. We might have taken a stand for God, followed the Spirit's leading to step out into an area of ministry, or curtailed an activity because of the Lord's conviction, and others don't understand. If we defend ourselves, things just seem to worsen and everywhere we turn we receive criticism and rejection. What did Mary do when she faced such circumstances? Nothing! She waited upon the Lord to vindicate her.

In the quietness of the night, God sent an angel to Joseph to confirm Mary's purity and His plan. While Mary and Joseph's situation was completely unique, I think we can learn a scriptural lesson from God's provision on their behalf: When you are doing the will of God, speak the truth, then let Him defend you. Even if we are able to vindicate ourselves with eloquence, there will always be those who refuse to believe the truth. Moses, Joseph, Isaiah, Stephen, Paul, and countless others through the ages experienced this. Being a Christian may mean being misunderstood, but it also means being in good company!

Scripture for Further Meditation:
But make up your mind not to worry
beforehand how you will defend yourselves.
For I will give you words and wisdom that
none of your adversaries will be able to
resist or contradict. Luke 21:14–15

Prayer:

Dear Father, I thank You that You are my
defender. Help me to be patient when I am
misunderstood and wait upon Your words and
wisdom for vindication. In Jesus' holy name.
Amen.

No Room

While they were there, the time came
for the baby to be born, and she gave birth
to her firstborn, a son. She wrapped Him in
cloths and placed Him in a manger, because
there was no room for them in the inn.
Luke 2:6–7

Have you ever thought about the blessings the
innkeeper missed? He had an opportunity to host the

most incredible event in history, and he refused. He could have been a witness to the coming of the Messiah, but he was too busy with his business. Because the holy family arrived unannounced and appeared unassuming, he sent them elsewhere. I wonder if he ever recognized the opportunity he allowed to slip through his fingers.

How easy it is to be like that innkeeper. When I get caught up in the demands of mothering and my life is filled with busywork, I often hang a "NO VACANCY" sign on my heart. How can I take time to read my Bible and pray when I have to be on the go from morning until night? If there are unoccupied pockets of time in my day, they are quickly filled with items plucked from my endless "to-do" list. The hours march by relentlessly, and I fall into bed with little more than a sighed prayer for the Lord to help me get some rest, so I can start all over in the morning! And then I wonder why I feel spiritually dry.

If the innkeeper had wanted to provide a place for Joseph and Mary, he could have. It would have meant, however, that he would have to move out one of his paying guests. It would have been inconvenient, but it would have created a space for the Savior. Isn't that the same option we each face as Christians every day? We too have the opportunity to make a place for Jesus to come into our lives. But in order to do so, we need to move out some of the things that currently occupy our time and energy. Maybe it will mean giving up some activities to make time for Bible study, getting up a little earlier in order to pray before beginning our day, separating ourselves from friends who are not a positive influence on our behavior.

Like the inn at Bethlehem, our lives are filled to overflowing with all sorts of demands. What will we do when the Savior comes knocking at the door? First we turn to God in repentance for neglecting His commandments, for hanging onto things that cause Him grief, for making excuses when we shove Him aside to make room for our own desires. Then we may ask the Lord Jesus to be born anew in us each day, as Martin Luther penned in his Christmas hymn, "Ah, dearest Jesus, holy child, make Thee a bed, soft, undefiled within my heart that it may be a quiet chamber kept for Thee."

Scripture for Further Meditation:
Here I am! I stand at the door and knock.
If anyone hears My voice and opens the door,
I will come in and eat with him, and he with
Me. Revelation 3:20

Prayer:

*Dear Jesus, forgive me when I am unwilling
for You to be Lord of my life. I desire to be
a witness of Your birth as You come to dwell
within me forever through Your Holy Spirit.
Thank You for the gift of eternal life that
You gave us through Your life, death,
and resurrection. Amen.*

Dedicated to God

*When the time of their purification
according to the Law of Moses had been
completed, Joseph and Mary took Him to
Jerusalem to present Him to the Lord
(as it is written in the Law of the Lord,
"Every firstborn male is to be consecrated
to the Lord"). Luke 2:22–23*

Joseph and Mary were very careful to do all they
could to obey God. It was their first priority. It didn't
matter if it was inconvenient, embarrassing, or didn't
make sense to anyone else. They were committed to
follow the Father. As they faced the daunting task of
raising God's only begotten Son, they recognized the

important responsibility they shared as Jesus' earthly parents. From the very beginning, they determined to raise their child according to the Book.

I wonder how different our homes might be if we shared this determination. So many of us look at our children as our possessions or as extensions of our own personalities. Dad wants Junior to succeed in sports as well as academics because that was Dad's dream as a boy. Mother wants her daughter to be beautiful and popular because those were Mom's goals as a girl. When we gather with other parents, we boast about our children's achievements as if they were our own and discuss their failures as if they were blots upon our own character. Children neither need nor want that kind of responsibility. It often breeds resentment and discouragement when they feel they have not lived up to our expectations.

How much better it is to adopt the attitude of Jesus' parents and dedicate our children to the Lord from the moment of their birth—or even before. Recognizing that each child is uniquely created by God with special strengths and weaknesses, talents and abilities, is a first step. Then we can pray to be used by God to help our sons and daughters become the individuals He wants each of them to be. Instead of making them over into "new and improved" models of ourselves, we can encourage them to develop into the persons God intended. As we help our children recognize and develop their own unique personalities, we have an opportunity to become partners with our heavenly Father in parenting.

Raising children is a daunting task and one that is too serious to be undertaken with our limited human resources. Joseph and Mary recognized this and acknowledged God's authority in their family from the very beginning. With a desire to raise godly children, we can do the same. Consecrating our little ones to God is a wonderful first step.

Scripture for Further Meditation:
Train a child in the way he should go,
and when he is old he will not turn from it.
Proverbs 22:6

Prayer:

Jesus, sometimes I am overwhelmed
at the responsibility of being a mother.
Please help me prayerfully to place my
children in Your hands each day, then
grant me wisdom as I carefully teach
and train them to follow You. Amen.

Love and Pain

> *Then Simeon blessed them and said to Mary,*
> *His mother: "This child is destined to cause*
> *the falling and rising of many in Israel, and*
> *to be a sign that will be spoken against, so*
> *that the thoughts of many hearts will be*
> *revealed. And a sword will pierce your*
> *own soul too. Luke 2:34–35*

Simeon's prophecy to Mary was not the happy sort of blessing one might hope to hear at a baby's dedication. It was downright frightening! But it was also very true. Given a vision of the future, the old prophet proclaimed that Jesus and Mary would be bound together by both love and pain.

Although most mothers do not have to see their children put to death, almost all of us experience the bittersweet blending of love and pain involved in mothering. From the very beginning we wrestle with both. The helplessness of a new baby causes our hearts to swell with love even as we realize how vulnerable she is to illness and injury. When we send our young ones off to school we experience loving pride, while at the same time we feel the pain of separation. Each developmental step and achievement increases our love for our children, yet hastens the day when they will leave our homes for good.

When Mary heard Simeon's message she could have refused to accept it, choosing instead to cloister

Jesus in a smothering environment intended to keep away all pain. But then she would not have been in obedience to God's plan for her or for her son. In order for Jesus to fulfill His mission, He needed to experience the life His Father had prepared for Him from the foundations of the earth—a life of both love and pain.

Our sons and daughters are not called to fulfill the same role as Mary's child, but they too have a mission in life. And that mission will inevitably bring both love and pain. To try to keep our children from the normal pains and disappointments of life will only prevent them from maturing into the adults God intends for them to be. To over-protect them so that we don't risk experiencing any pain is damaging to both parent and child. Trusting that God, in His sovereignty, knows what lies ahead for us as well as our children, enables us to embrace both the love and pain essential to growth.

Scripture for Further Meditation:
For I am convinced that neither death nor life,
neither angels nor demons, neither the present
nor the future, nor any powers, neither height
nor depth, nor anything else in all creation,
will be able to separate us from the love
of God that is in Christ Jesus our Lord.
Romans 8:38–39

*I thank You, Jesus, for caring enough about
me to allow me to grow through both love and
pain. May my children see in me a reflection
of You that encourages them through all the
challenges of growing up. Amen.*

Daily Devotion

*When Joseph and Mary had done everything
required by the Law of the Lord, they returned
to Galilee to their own town of Nazareth.
And the child grew and became strong;
He was filled with wisdom, and the grace
of God was upon Him. Luke 2:39–40*

There are hundreds of books on child rearing
available to parents. Some offer radical methods of
teaching toddlers to read and do math. Some extol
the classics and music while others focus on emotional development. One expert suggests firm limits
and swift discipline for misbehavior and another
urges a tolerant response for youthful indiscretions.
Without such abundant resources, Joseph and Mary
raised Jesus with confidence and consistency. How

did they manage it?

We are told in the Scriptures that Mary and Joseph had their priorities straight. The first thing they did was to make sure that they were obedient to God in their own areas of responsibility. They fulfilled their roles as defined by Scripture. Then they provided Jesus with a home obviously filled with love. In response to this environment, the Bible tells us, as Jesus matured He was balanced physically, emotionally, socially, intellectually, and spiritually.

I suspect that the daily fabric of Jesus' life was embroidered with devotion to God, responsibility to community, and respect to family. We know both Joseph and Mary were individuals who prayed and worshiped God regularly. We also see from their actions prior to Jesus' birth that they each possessed integrity, sensitivity, and humility. They were attentive to the voice of the Lord and swift to obey. In our desire to be parents who raise godly children, we can first nourish our personal relationship with our Savior. This requires time spent studying Scripture, praying, worshiping, and living according to our professed faith. We cannot expect our children to adopt a lifestyle and values we do not demonstrate.

With our own lives in line with God, it is easier to raise our children according to His will. Consistent, daily attention to how our children are growing in all aspects of development allows us to see when their lives might be out of balance. Are they spending too much time with physical activities, not enough with academics? Is there an emotional strain that's sapping their strength or a health problem that needs care? What proportion of their day is spent with family, with friends, in quiet time with the Lord, or engaged in service to others? Good parenting isn't so much a matter of finding the one right technique as it is of providing daily guidance that helps our sons and daughters move in the right direction—becoming strong, wise, and responsive to God's grace.

Scripture for Further Meditation:
Fix these words of Mine in your hearts and minds; tie them as symbols on your hands and bind them on your foreheads. Teach them to your children, talking about them when you sit at home and when you walk along the road, when you lie down and when you get up. Deuteronomy 11:18–19

Prayer:

Dear Jesus, I desire to be a good parent, to raise my children according to Your Word and will. Help me to follow You so I may be a good example. Please give me the strength to daily devote myself to teach and train my children. Amen.

Letting Go

*Then Jesus entered a house, and again a
crowd gathered, so that He and His disciples
were not even able to eat. When His family
heard about this, they went to take charge
of Him, for they said, "He is out of His mind."*
Mark 3:20–21

No matter how much we love our children, there
will come a time when we may not understand them,
agree with their choices, or even approve of what
they do. As parents it is tempting to believe we know
what is best for our kids. And when they're young,
this is probably true. But as they mature and develop
their unique talents and gifts, they often take paths
unfamiliar to us. When this happens, it can be difficult for us as parents.

Look at the situation in Jesus' family. After 30
years living at home in Nazareth with His parents,
half-brothers, and half-sisters, Jesus began His public
ministry. Until that time, as far as we know, He lived
a normal, unremarkable life as a carpenter's son. (It
is assumed by many that His carpentry may have provided support for the family after Joseph's death.)
Then He had a sudden career change. He left home,
gathered a group of strangers as His friends, and traveled from town to town healing the sick and performing other miracles. Crowds gathered to hear Him
teach. The respectable elders of the synagogue

accused Him of law breaking and blasphemy. Some even considered Him possessed by Satan!

After learning all of this, it's not surprising that His relatives headed out to find Him and bring Him home for some rest and recuperation. The Bible says they thought He was crazy! They assumed they knew what was best for Jesus because they loved Him and they were His family.

When our grown children choose a career path or life partner we might not have chosen, it is tempting for us, just as it was for Mary, to rush in and try to rescue them from what we see as a potential disaster. But God may not be directing them down the same path He directed us. He might have a new work for them, a totally new direction. Their world is not ours, and ultimately we must relinquish our control over them.

Jesus' family didn't understand that their dreams and ambitions were not Jesus' own. They had to let Him go to fulfill God's plan for His life. We too must let our children go at some point, continually trusting them to the Lord's care. God loves our children and will guide them, but often we need to step back and take a supporting role. We can pray for them, offer advice when asked, and be there if they need us. But if we desire to maintain a healthy relationship with our grown kids, we need to be willing to let them fulfill their own destiny—even if what they're doing makes little sense to us.

Scripture for Further Meditation:
Show me Your ways, O LORD, teach me Your paths; guide me in Your truth and teach me, for You are God my Savior, and my hope is in You all day long. Psalm 25:4–5

Prayer:

Dear Lord, I know You are able to direct my children in the paths You have chosen for them. Keep them ever mindful of Your direction and help me to be a supportive and wise parent as I relinquish my grown children into Your loving care. In Jesus' name and for His sake. Amen.

Prayer Warrior

They all joined together constantly in prayer, along with the women and Mary the mother of Jesus, and His brothers. Acts 1:14

Mary's life was one of prayer. From the time she is introduced in Scripture, speaking with the angel Gabriel, we see her worshiping, praising, and pondering her heavenly Father. Although we often think of her as a simple peasant woman, she possessed a wisdom that surpassed education and social station. And that wisdom drew her to a life of continual prayer. Think of the daunting task given her: to raise the only begotten Son of God. Consider the emotional price she paid: standing by as her beloved son is misunderstood, misinterpreted, betrayed, and finally executed as a common criminal. And still she prayed.

Few of us will ever be called upon to witness our own offspring endure so much, but all mothers know the frustration of watching our children suffer. Sometimes it is a physical trial of injury or disease. Perhaps it is an emotional trauma or psychological disorder. At one time or another it may be social difficulties that affect our kids. Whatever the situation, there will be times when we can do nothing but fall on our knees and raise our children before God in prayer.

What Mary's example illustrates is the importance of praying constantly for our children from their youngest years on. We commune with God, seeking His wisdom and direction as we care for our little ones, and He directs us. We send them out of the home to school or play, and He calms our fears and gives us confidence to trust in His loving care. As they face the temptations of adolescence, He reassures us that His hand is upon them. When they leave home for college and careers, we know He will never leave them or forsake them. And even if they move far away from us physically, we can experience a closeness of the heart as we lift them daily before the throne of God in prayer.

I once heard a mother say of her rebellious child, "He can refuse to listen to my words. He can avoid having a conversation with me. He can choose to move out. He can tell me I'm nuts. But he can't make me stop praying for him!" Prayer is a mother's first, last, and best weapon in the arsenal of parenting. In prayer we touch the heart of God, and our own hearts are opened to be touched in return. In prayer we realize the power of the Holy Spirit to work in and through us. In prayer we bring those we love to God and receive the peace of knowing they are in the Father's hands.

Scripture for Further Meditation:
And pray in the Spirit on all occasions with all kinds of prayers and requests. With this in mind, be alert and always keep on praying for all the saints. Ephesians 6:18

Prayer:

Dear Father, I thank You for the example of Mary's prayer life. And I ask that You would enable me to be a prayer warrior for my children. Help me to learn the discipline of daily prayer, lifting their joys and concerns to You, knowing that You care for them even more than I can. Amen.

Other Mothers
from the
New Testament

WE ARE MOTHERS who lived during and after the time of Christ. Some of us are old and some very young. Many of us walked with the Master through the dusty streets of Judea, but others of us never met Him face to face. We heard about Him, though, and believed in His power to help our children.

There was little hope for children in the days when we lived. Death and disease were ever-present enemies, waiting greedily for an opportunity to snatch our little ones from us. Many of us were poor and had no means to seek the help of doctors. We used the medicine of superstition and mother's love because we had nothing else. Then word came of One who could heal with a touch, raise the dead to life again, unstop tongues, and free the mind from demons. *Could it be?* we wondered. We carried our dying children to Him, hoping the stories weren't just the work of rumor and imagination. And what we found was truth. Some of us saw our crippled children walk again. Some stood amazed as our sons looked upon us for the very first time. One set a meal before her daughter who, only moments earlier, had known the grip of death. Our hearts nearly burst with joy as we saw our broken children restored and whole. And we returned to our homes praising God.

Some of us brought our little ones to Jesus just so He could touch and bless them. The disciples tried to push us away, telling us their Master was busy with other, more important things. But Jesus saw us, looked into our eyes, and knew our thoughts. He took our little ones and held them. He smiled at them and stroked their hair. And then He taught us all that to enter into His kingdom we must become like a child—humble and trusting and willing to believe in God's love for us.

Those of us who never met Jesus heard of Him through others. We listened as Peter, Paul, John, and Barnabas told us how the Master lived and how He died. But most important, they told us how He rose from death and conquered sin. We learned we—and our children—could be saved from lives of emptiness and despair. In prayer we trusted God's Son and taught our children so they might know also the abundant life He promised and live as God's children now and in eternity.

At last we knew there was hope beyond the small confines of our weary lives. There was healing for both soul and body at the cross of Christ. We had little to give our children before we knew the Savior, but after He came we had the riches of God at our disposal. Is it any wonder that as mothers we came to adore Jesus? We saw in Him the love that had created our children, and the only love that could sustain them for all eternity. 🌸

At Your Service

When Jesus came into Peter's house,
He saw Peter's mother-in-law lying in bed
with a fever. He touched her hand and the
fever left her, and she got up and began
to wait on Him. Matthew 8:14–15

Most of us wouldn't want anyone to show up at our door when we're not feeling well. Aching and in bed with a fever, I suspect Peter's mother-in-law felt the same way. That is until she discovered it was Jesus who had stopped in for a visit. When Jesus comes into our lives, everything changes! Notice the progression in these verses: Jesus came in, He saw the sick woman, He touched her, she was renewed, and she began to serve the Savior.

In a sense, the story of this mother is the story of each of us. The hurried pace of our lives, the burden of responsibilities, the weight of depression, or the disabling effects of a disease can strike us down like a fever. We feel overwhelmed and ineffective, unable to carry on with our normal routines. It is at these times that Jesus comes to call, seeking entrance to our "sickroom." He doesn't stand outside, like a polite and distant acquaintance, but makes Himself at home, immediately seeing what is wrong, understanding our pain, and desiring to help.

I suspect Jesus and this mother were not strangers. Perhaps they had often visited before and maybe Jesus was a frequent guest at Peter's home. Although no words are spoken, there is an understanding of love between the two; the kind of love that reflects a comfortable relationship. Jesus doesn't wait after He is told of her illness to go to her, nor does He ask her what she wants. Instead, moved by compassion, He sees her need and touches her. It is in this touch that we see the power of Christ to transform sickness into health, weakness to strength, darkness to light. This is the same power God makes available to all His children. Sometimes we see it in the restoration of relationships. At other times it is evident in the renewal of hope. Sometimes it takes the form of physical or emotional healing. Whenever Jesus touches us, we experience the power of His love—a love that raises and restores.

But notice how Peter's mother-in-law responds to the love of Christ. She "got up and began to wait upon Him." What do we do after we have received a special touch from Jesus? Do we use our renewed strength to continue in our own pursuits, or do we seek to discover how we might serve the Savior? While Jesus' love is extended to each of us in personal and private ways, the Gospel imperative is that we can reach out to others with the same healing touch we have received from God. As mothers we have a great need to be renewed and restored by Christ daily, so we may serve Him with the strength He gives.

Scripture for Further Meditation:
Serve wholeheartedly, as if you were serving the
Lord, not men, because you know that the Lord
will reward everyone for whatever good he does,
whether he is slave or free. Ephesians 6:7–8

Prayer:

Dear Jesus, I thank You for the loving way
You touch my life, giving me strength when
I am weak. Help me to use my energy to serve
You as I minister to my family, church, and
community. Let me be Your hands and feet,
bringing help to those You love. Amen.

Obstinate Faith

A Canaanite woman from that vicinity came to
Him, crying out, "Lord, Son of David, have mercy
on me! My daughter is suffering terribly from
demon-possession." ... The woman came and knelt
before Him. "Lord, help me!" she said ... "Yes,
Lord," she said, "but even the dogs eat the crumbs
that fall from their masters' table." Then Jesus
answered, "Woman, you have great faith. Your
request is granted." Matthew 15:22, 25, 27–28

After a busy period of ministry, Jesus and His disciples withdrew to a region north of Galilee near the seacoast. They probably wanted to be alone to reflect on the events of the past few days. But there was a problem. A pagan woman from the region heard about Jesus, and she was badly in need of a miracle for her demon-possessed daughter. She had never met the Master, she wasn't a Jew, and she had no credentials or money to offer. All she had was a mother's love and a desperate need. Ignoring the irritated stares and rebukes of the disciples, she persistently called out to Jesus.

Surprisingly, Jesus did not answer. The disciples, seeing her get in the way of their retreat, asked Jesus to send her away. Jesus told them, "I was sent only to the lost sheep of Israel." Refusing to be discouraged, the woman threw herself before Christ pleading for help. In what might sound to our ears an unfeeling response, Jesus verbally sparred with the mother, using a metaphor to explain His position: "It is not right to take the children's bread and toss it to their dogs." Far from being dissuaded, the woman turned the metaphor to her own purposes and suggested she would be satisfied with only the crumbs from the Savior's hands. The honest humility and depth of her faith delighted Jesus as He announced to all that her request was granted. Scripture reports that "her daughter was healed from that very hour."

What would it take for us to demonstrate this kind

of God-pleasing faith? First, we need to know that God's silence is not God's *no* and that Jesus is able to do what we ask. Second, we pray earnestly, worshiping God and seeking His mercy to prevail in our situation. Third, we persist even when circumstances and others seemingly conspire to discourage us. This is obstinate faith, the kind demonstrated by the mother from Canaan; the kind of faith Jesus praised. The Lord can and will increase our faith if we but ask.

Scripture for Further Meditation:
Jesus replied, "I tell you the truth, if you have faith and do not doubt, not only can you do what was done to the fig tree, but also you can say to this mountain, 'Go, throw yourself into the sea,' and it will be done. If you believe, you will receive whatever you ask for in prayer."
Matthew 21:21–22

Prayer:

Dear Lord, I long to have mountain-moving faith. Help me to be persistent in prayer, unwavering in my belief, and single-minded in purpose, so I might please You and be a channel of blessing to others. In Jesus' name I pray. Amen.

Blind Ambition

Then the mother of Zebedee's sons came
to Jesus with her sons and, kneeling down,
asked a favor of Him. "What is it you want?"
He asked. She said, "Grant that one of these
two sons of mine may sit at Your right and
the other at Your left in Your kingdom."
Matthew 20:20–21

What's wrong with wanting the best for our children? It certainly sounds like a noble cause. But to what lengths are we willing to go? What sacrifices are we prepared to make? Some families relocate so their children can have access to better schools, coaches, or training facilities. Some parents work two or more jobs to earn enough money to provide private school tuition or money for music, dancing, or other expensive lessons. Retirement accounts are emptied to pay for college tuition at prestigious universities so Junior can have a better chance at grad school. Although we may maintain we only want what's best for our kids, it often boils down to getting them preferential treatment. Like the mother of James and John, we want everyone to know how special our children are, and we are willing to go to great lengths to secure special treatment for them.

Although these sacrifices sound noble, sometimes we are guilty of trading the integrity of our family to fulfill our own selfish ambitions. As parents we know that the accomplishments of our children are often seen as a reflection of our own success. We don't hear too many mothers bragging about Johnny's average athletic achievements or Susie's last C in history. It is easy to get our children's worth, and our own, confused with the way the world views success.

In a way, that's what Salome, the mother of James and John, was doing. She knew her sons had been plucked from relative obscurity at the Galilean fishing docks to become members of the Messiah's inner circle. But what about the kingdom to come? After all, the Messiah only had two sides, and she only had two sons. She'd better speak up for them or they might miss out on a great opportunity! Her blind ambition on behalf of her sons caused her to miss the main point about Christ's kingdom: It is not of this world! (See John 18:36.) Jesus' kingdom is not governed by the world's standards of greatness. In fact He repeatedly told His followers that in His kingdom they must become poor to become rich, less to become more, and humble to become great.

In Jesus' response to this ambitious mother, He reveals that there is only One who confers places of honor in the kingdom to come: "These places belong to those for whom they have been prepared by my Father." And in that statement lies the warning for all of us mothers when we're tempted to push our kids into the spotlight: True greatness comes only from God.

Scripture for Further Meditation:

The greatest among you will be your servant.
For whoever exalts himself will be humbled,
and whoever humbles himself will be exalted.
Matthew 23:11–12

Prayer:

Thank You, Father, for the privilege of being
a mother. Please forgive me when my ego
gets in the way of what You want to
accomplish for and through my children.
Help me teach them that their priceless
worth is based on being a child of God,
not on any earthly honor or position.
In Jesus' holy name. Amen.

Faithful to the End

Many women were there, watching from a
distance. They had followed Jesus from Galilee
to care for His needs. Among them were Mary
Magdalene, Mary the mother of James and
Joses, and the mother of Zebedee's sons.
Matthew 27:55–56

In his last days on earth, our Savior experienced betrayal from one of His closest associates, false accusations from the leaders of His own people, abandonment by nearly all of His disciples, and denial by one who had promised to die for Him. Yet there were some who never left Him. And among that tiny group, gathered at the foot of the cross, were several mothers.

John tells us that Jesus' mother, Mary, was there (John 19:25), but Matthew names three additional women who were present. And they were not only present at the moment of His death, they had followed Jesus from Galilee, caring for His needs. Perhaps they prepared meals for the Messiah and His followers or maybe they washed their garments or repaired their worn sandals. Scripture is silent on the exact nature of their service, but it is clear that they remained true to Jesus despite the dangers of being associated with Him.

This is a beautiful model for all of us to follow today. There are many times when it may not be easy or convenient to follow Christ, but there is always work to be done. Sometimes the tasks He requires may not be glamorous, but they serve to further the kingdom and spread the Gospel. At times being a member of Christ's kingdom will lead us into uncomfortable situations, yet that may be the very place where God can use us best. There will be times to be active and also times to wait patiently and prayerfully for God's leading.

As mothers we know firsthand the requirements of love and as mothers we are also uniquely equipped to share that love. Perhaps that is why so many mothers stood on that lonely hillside outside Jerusalem, remaining faithful to the end. Written in their hearts were the words that would be penned in Scripture years later by the apostle Paul: "[Love] always protects, always trusts, always hopes, always perseveres" (1 Corinthians 13:7).

Scripture for Further Meditation:
Let love and faithfulness never leave you;
bind them around your neck, write them
on the tablet of your heart. Then you will
win favor and a good name in the sight
of God and man. Proverbs 3:3–4

Prayer:

Dear Lord Jesus, I thank You that You
were faithful to endure the cross on
my account. Please grant me the courage
to raise my children with integrity and
the strength to remain faithful to You
all my days. In Your name. Amen.

Without Hope

While Jesus was still speaking, some men came from the house of Jairus, the synagogue ruler. "Your daughter is dead," they said. "Why bother the teacher any more?" Ignoring what they said, Jesus told the synagogue ruler, "Don't be afraid; just believe." Mark 5:35–36

Jairus and his wife were up against a wall. Their beloved 12-year-old daughter was gravely ill. None of the doctors they knew could help her. They had one option left, but to take it might risk Jairus' career and their position in the community. Jairus was a leader in the local synagogue, and his colleagues were skeptical of Jesus of Nazareth, the one some hailed as the Son of God. Yet these parents had heard that Jesus had power to heal the sick, even control the forces of nature. Their daughter was dying, and He was their only hope.

While the mother stayed home with their daughter, Jairus hurried to beg Jesus for help. Just when it seemed things couldn't get any worse, they did. Before her husband could return, Jairus' wife sat helplessly as life ebbed from her daughter. Grief-stricken, she announced the girl's death to the attending family and friends. Soon loud wails of anguish filled the court-yard, and the mother wept alone and without hope, feeling abandoned by both man and God.

It was at this moment Jesus arrived. Ignoring the mourners and those who claimed He was too late,

Jesus took the father, mother, and three disciples into the girl's chamber. There, taking the child by the hand, He commanded her to get up. Miraculously she not only stood, but walked around, and Jesus told them to give her something to eat. Once more He had proved His power over life and death, the triumph of hope over despair.

Many mothers know the hopelessness of Jairus' wife. They may sit beside a bed in a hospital ward, watching as their child loses her battle with cancer. They may grieve in a courtroom as their child is convicted of a crime and sent to jail. They may experience the anguish of committing a son or daughter into the care of a mental hospital or drug rehab center. At those times it is easy to believe God doesn't care, or has arrived too late to help. It is easy to lose heart and lose hope.

It is then that the words of Jesus, spoken to Jairus centuries ago, can take root in our hearts: "Don't be afraid; just believe." Whether in this life or the next, Jesus has the ultimate power to heal and restore life. In His sovereignty He knows what is best and promises to come to us and stand beside us in our darkest hour. In Christ there is always hope.

Scripture for Further Meditation:
May the God of hope fill you with all joy
and peace as you trust in Him, so that
you may overflow with hope by the power
of the Holy Spirit. Romans 15:13

Prayer:

*Lord Jesus, You are my hope and in You
I believe. Help me to keep my eyes on
You, not the circumstances that surround
me. When I feel hopeless, fill me with
Your Spirit and give me strength to face
whatever happens knowing that ultimately
You triumph over sickness and death.
In your name I pray. Amen.*

Bringing Little Ones to Christ

*People were bringing little children to Jesus
to have Him touch them, but the disciples
rebuked them. When Jesus saw this,
He was indignant. He said to them,
"Let the little children come to Me, and
do not hinder them, for the kingdom of God
belongs to such as these." Mark 10:13–14*

Looking around at the crowds clamoring for Jesus, the disciples must have felt protective of their Master's time and energy. Perhaps they established a sort of spiritual "triage" where seekers were categorized according to the seriousness of their apparent needs: paralytics over here, blind folks keep to the right, lepers wait in the back, and so on. In their assessment, the people with children, hoping only for a touch of blessing for their little ones, were at the bottom of the list. Couldn't these mothers and others with crying tots see that Jesus had really important work to do? But, the Scriptures tell us, the actions and attitudes of the disciples filled Jesus with indignation! He told the impatient adults that the kingdom of God is made up of those with childlike trust and then, in a pronouncement affirming the inestimable value of little children, Jesus opened His arms and gathered them to Himself.

How often are we like those disciples? Oh, we love and protect our children, but we underestimate their ability to develop a meaningful spiritual relationship with Christ. We view Sunday school more as baby-sitting than as an opportunity to teach biblical truths. We hesitate to volunteer to help in the nursery or teach vacation Bible school. In our homes, we spend more time reading popular children's literature and fairy tales to our children than we do sharing Bible stories. We drill our youngsters on math facts and state capitals, yet neglect the memorization of Scripture verses. In a way, don't these kinds of attitudes and actions give our children the same message as the disciples? Aren't we saying, "Come back to see Jesus when you're older. He doesn't have time for you now."

In truth, children often have a clearer and simpler view of spiritual truths than adults. Uninhibited by prejudice and worldly sophistication, they eagerly grasp biblical teachings. If we agree with child psychologists that the moral and ethical foundation for life is well-established by the age of 6, shouldn't we be doing all we can in those early years to bring our little ones to know and love Jesus and to know how much He loves them? As mothers we have a priceless opportunity to teach our children of the Savior by our words, our attitudes, and our actions. It doesn't mean we can live perfect lives, but that by the power of the Holy Spirit, we must be willing to live out our faith on a daily basis, providing a model for our sons and daughters. It is our privilege to bring them to the arms of Jesus.

Scripture for Further Meditation:
We will tell the next generation the praiseworthy deeds of the LORD, His power and the wonders He has done … so the next generation would know them, even the children yet to be born, and they in turn would tell their children. Then they would put their trust in God and would not forget His deeds but would keep His commands. Psalm 78:4b, 6–7

rayer:

*Dear Lord, help me to seize every possible
opportunity to tell little ones of You. Whether
in my own family or in my community and
church, help me to reach out with Your love
to children, sharing with them the wonderful
Gospel of Your saving grace for us in Jesus.
Amen.*

A Sorrowful Heart

*As He approached the town gate, a dead
person was being carried out—the only
son of his mother, and she was a widow.
And a large crowd from the town was with her.
When the Lord saw her, His heart went out
to her and He said, "Don't cry." Luke 7:12–13*

There are times when we feel all alone with our
sorrow. It seems there is no one who understands or
cares about what we are enduring. Friends may have
good intentions, but their comfort is limited. Such
was the case with the widow of Nain.

At that time, a woman's worth depended upon her
husband's position in the town where they lived. He

supported and defended the family, providing what-ever security they enjoyed. If he became disabled or died, the eldest son took over the care for his mother, ensuring her ability to survive within the community. Widowed and having just lost her only son, this poor woman faced a life of poverty and dependence upon the charity of others. And then she met Jesus.

Accompanied by His disciples and a large crowd of followers, Jesus approached the gate of Nain just as the funeral procession for the widow's son left the town. Although death was a common occurrence in first-century Galilee, Jesus did not view this scene as an opportunity to preach about the brevity of life or to give a sermon on the kingdom of God. Jesus saw a poor widow who had lost her only child, and His heart went out to her. In compassion He told her to cease her weeping and then, in holy power, He brought her son back to life.

While the miraculous raising of the widow's son is usually the primary focus of this passage, there is another, quieter miracle that takes place first. It is the miracle that the Creator and Sustainer of the universe would walk along the same road as a poor widow, would recognize the depth of her pain, and would reach out to her in compassion. What a comfort it is to know that we serve a God who does not distance Himself from us. When we walk through the valley of the shadow of death, He is right there with us. When our hearts ache with pain too deep for words, His

heart reaches out to us. When we think no one understands or has compassion for us, He whispers, "Don't
cry." Jesus tenderly touches us with His love when
we are too blinded by grief and tears to even realize
He is there. When our hopes and dreams seem life-
less, He stretches out His hand to restore us with His
life-giving power.

Scripture for Further Meditation:
Praise be to the God and Father of our Lord
Jesus Christ, the Father of compassion and the
God of all comfort, who comforts us in all our
troubles, so that we can comfort those in any
trouble with the comfort we ourselves have
received from God. 2 Corinthians 1:3–4

Prayer:

Dear Jesus, I thank You for the miracle
of Your love that seeks me out and ministers
to me. Help me recognize Your touch in
the midst of my pain and respond to You
with renewed faith and hope.
In Your holy name I pray. Amen.

The Grip of Guilt

As He went along, He saw a man
blind from birth. His disciples asked Him,
"Rabbi, who sinned, this man or his parents,
that he was born blind?" "Neither this man
nor his parents sinned," said Jesus,
"but this happened so that the work
of God might be displayed in his life."
John 9:1–3

When a friend of mine gave birth to her third son, it was evident from the subdued tone of the doctors in the delivery room that something was wrong with the baby. Within a few weeks, pediatric specialists had determined the tiny boy had a serious and untreatable neurological disorder. Although the child would probably survive, the doctors told the parents that their son was severely mentally disabled and would never sit up, walk, feed himself, or speak. The little boy is now 5 and the doctors' grim prognosis has proved to be true.

My friend and her husband are strong believers in Jesus Christ. Yet she reports that for the first few months after her son's diagnosis, she questioned God's love. Then, she said, the inquiries of others, their constant probing for reasons and causes, led her to fall into a dark pit of guilt. She wondered if something she had done—or not done—during her pregnancy was to blame for her son's condition. After much prayer and guidance in a Bible study, she said she was finally released from the grip of guilt as she recognized that God had neither turned against her nor punished her through her son. In fact she began to realize that her family's situation could become an opportunity to praise and glorify God. Each day, she reminds herself that it is God's strength that enables her to meet new challenges. She takes time to visit with and pray for other mothers of disabled children. She participates in the life of her church, and her testimony of Christ's unfailing power in the midst of difficulties has encouraged several individuals to trust the Savior. She witnessed firsthand the work of God displayed through the life of her little boy.

In the Scripture passage from Luke, the disciples asked the very human question: Who's to blame? They believed birth defects and misfortune were the result of sin—not the general sin of a fallen world, but the specific sin of an individual. They wanted to fix blame and assign guilt. Often we want to do the same thing. We ask "Why?" when disease or disability strikes. But God gently reminds us, as He did the curious disciples, that He doesn't always work according to our understanding, but in accordance with His purposes. When we are tempted to assign blame or assume guilt for things over which we have no control, Jesus calls us to remember that often it is through the difficult places in life that God is able to accomplish His finest work.

Scripture for Further Meditation:
But He said to me, "My grace is sufficient for you, for My power is made perfect in weakness." Therefore I will boast all the more gladly about my weaknesses, so that Christ's power may rest on me. That is why, for Christ's sake, I delight in weaknesses, in insults, in hardships, in persecutions, in difficulties. For when I am weak, then I am strong. 2 Corinthians 12:9–10

Prayer:

Father, I do not always understand the things that happen in my life, but I trust that You have a plan for me that cannot be thwarted. Help me to trust in You and to live each day confident that You are at work accomplishing Your purposes through me. Free me from inappropriate guilt so that I might bring glory to your Son. In His name I pray. Amen.

Don't Ask Me

> *"We know he is our son," the parents answered,*
> *"and we know he was born blind. But how*
> *he can see now, or who opened his eyes,*
> *we don't know. Ask him."* ... *His parents said*
> *this because they were afraid of the Jews, for*
> *already the Jews had decided that anyone who*
> *acknowledged that Jesus was the Christ would*
> *be put out of the synagogue. John 9:20–21a, 22*

Have you ever felt as if you were being put on the spot? You're at a social function, and conversation swirls around, dancing from topic to topic. Then someone asks a direct question requiring an answer that will set you apart as a Christian. The room grows quiet and faces turn toward you expectantly. You assess your audience, quickly noting the people you might offend or alienate with your answer; your heart pounds and your palms sweat. Then you open your mouth.

It's easy to stand up for Christ in a friendly environment such as church or a Bible study group. We know we'll be encouraged and affirmed. But it takes courage to speak up when we're out of our comfort zone. What will people think? Will this have a negative impact upon my relationships or my job? What if I take a stand and then can't defend my position adequately? How may of us are truly comfortable taking these kinds of risks? While we admire the confidence of Stephen, the boldness of Paul, and the conviction of Peter, most of us prefer to avoid the possibility of rejection because of our faith. We may not praise the mother of the blind man, but if we're honest, most of us can understand her.

Why wouldn't she speak up and praise Jesus for healing her son? For the same reason many of us hedge when asked about our faith. Her fear of the people around her was greater than her confidence in Christ. After all, the synagogue leaders held great power and she knew what they could do to those who defied them. God might be able to heal her son, but dealing with these men was different. Sometimes we feel the same way. We see God accomplish great things for others, but doubt that He can deal with the problems in our own life. In our doubt and fear we deny the very faith we claim to hold so precious. If we are to develop boldness for Christ, we don't need to rehearse eloquent theological speeches. Instead, we need to confess our stumbling trust, to saturate ourselves in the Word so we grow in our daily dependence upon God to supply all our needs—even to provide the words when we're put on the spot!

Scripture for Further Meditation:
But when they arrest you, do not worry about what to say or how to say it. At that time you will be given what to say, for it will not be you speaking, but the Spirit of your Father speaking through you. Matthew 10:19–20

 *rayer:*

*Dear Father, I confess I am not always
bold to speak up for You. Forgive my fears
and my silence. Give me the courage to
defend my faith in ways that will bring
glory to Your name. I thank You that
You have given me the Holy Spirit
as a teacher and helper. Amen.*

Open-Door Policy

*When this had dawned on [Peter] he went
to the house of Mary, the mother of John,
also called Mark, where many people had
gathered and were praying. Acts 12:12*

It was a perilous time in the life of the early
church and association with followers of Jesus could
land one in prison—or worse. Loss of position and
property along with persecution were very real possi-
bilities. Yet in the fellowship of believers there were
those who risked everything for the cause of Christ.
One of these was Mary, the mother of John Mark.

Mary had a lot to lose. She was a wealthy woman,
owning a large home in a good neighborhood. She

had servants and occupied a position of respect in her community. How easy it would have been for her to hide behind the double walls of her home, to protect herself and her family from the dangers of Herod's spies.

But Mary had an open door policy. She welcomed displaced believers into her home. She entertained disciples as well as seekers, providing a place where they could meet, pray, and encourage one another in the Lord. And all the while her son, John Mark, observed not only his mother's personal commitment but her willingness to put herself at risk for the body of Christ.

When Peter was arrested, Mary hosted a prayer vigil lasting for several days on behalf of the imprisoned apostle. And after Peter's miraculous release from Herod's prison, the freed man hurried to Mary's home to share the story of God's deliverance. He knew the faithful would be gathered there.

Because of his mother's courageous hospitality, John Mark spent his youth in the company of the leadership of the early church. Missionaries, apostles, and disciples were his companions and mentors. His mind and heart were no doubt filled with tales of God's provision for the growing church. It is little wonder that when Barnabas and Paul decided to include an apprentice in their missionary travels, John Mark was eager to go.

Today it is easy to become involved in the local

church, yet keep our home life separate and private. If we want to expose our children to the personal lives of other believers, however, we can open our homes in hospitality to the followers of Christ. Hosting Bible studies, small groups, or prayer circles and inviting pastors or visiting missionaries to dinner provide opportunities for our children to become better acquainted with the Lord's work in its many facets. Getting to know about different careers in full time Christian service may even inspire a future pastor, teacher, or other church worker! An open door policy to the people of God may cost personal time, social position, and privacy, but the enriching benefits are priceless.

Scripture for Further Meditation:
Share with God's people who are in need. Practice hospitality. Romans 12:13

Prayer:

Dear Father, thank You for our family and the local fellowship of believers to which we belong. Help us to open our doors to the people of God, welcoming them with Christian hospitality into our hearts and home. In Jesus' name. Amen.

A Mother to Others

Greet Rufus, chosen in the Lord, and his mother,
who has been a mother to me, too. Romans 16:13

I was browsing through the card rack looking for
a Mother's Day card when I found a section of greet-
ings for "Someone who has been like a mother to
me." Is seems even the card companies recognize the
important role played by women who share their
mothering with those who are not their own children.

When I was a newlywed living thousands of miles
from home, I recall an older woman in our apartment
building who took me under her wing. She taught me
how to cook chicken enchiladas and bake Texas sheet
cake. But the most important thing she did for me
was to listen. She let me share my anxieties and my
dreams. She graciously helped me untangle the curious mazes of military protocol and laughed with me
over my frequent misconceptions and ineptitude. She
served as a substitute mother, generously sharing her
time and her wisdom. I corresponded with her regularly for the next 25 years and, when she passed
away, I felt as if I had lost a member of the family.

Whether we are close to our own mothers or not,
there are times when other mothers fill the empty
places in our lives. Perhaps they have expertise in an
area where we lack insights. They may have experiences with the kinds of difficulties we are facing.
Because of their objectivity they may be able to help

us face our own areas of weakness and immaturity and help us change in positive ways.

It is clear that Rufus' mother was a woman who opened both her heart and home to the apostle Paul. As missionaries to and from the early church traveled through Rome in the latter part of the first century, they probably knew to stop at her home for a good meal and a safe night's rest. By allowing herself to be a blessing to others, she widened her family circle and welcomed the young men and women of the early church as her own sons and daughters. The family of God is not limited by our human parentage, but expanded to include those to whom we are related by the blood of Christ our Savior.

Scripture for Further Meditation:

He replied, "Who is My mother, and who are My brothers?" Pointing to His disciples, He said, "Here are My mother and My brothers. For whoever does the will of My Father in heaven is My brother and sister and mother." Matthew 12:48–50

Prayer:

Dear Jesus, thank You for making me a part of Your family. Help me to extend the boundaries of my human family to include those who need the touch of a mother or a daughter and give me a heart to reach out to others with Your love. Amen.

Tender Teachers

I have been reminded of your sincere faith,
which first lived in your grandmother Lois and
in your mother Eunice and, I am persuaded,
now lives in you also. 2 Timothy 1:5

It is interesting to note that the word "grandmother" only appears once in Scripture. In that instance, quoted above in Paul's letter to Timothy, the influential teaching of the young man's grandmother and mother is noted as the birthplace of Timothy's sincere faith. What a confirmation of the importance of a mother's role!

If we read further in this letter to Timothy, we learn that this mother and grandmother did not wait until he was a youth to begin his training in the ways of the Lord: "But as for you, continue in what you have learned and have become convinced of, because you know those from whom you learned it, and how from infancy you have known the holy Scriptures, which are able to make you wise for salvation through faith in Christ Jesus" (2 Timothy 3:14–15).

It is safe to assume that Lois was a woman of God, acquainted with the teachings of the Old Testament. When she raised her daughter, Eunice, she no doubt taught her the love of God, the principles of faith, and obedience to God, duty to husband and family, loyalty to the people of faith. We know from Acts that Timothy's father was a Greek and apparently not involved in his religious training. Therefore, it was this legacy of maternal faith that transmitted to Timothy the truths of God. From his infancy the little boy heard the words of the Lord spoken and explained. His mother and grandmother may have sung the psalms to him as they rocked him to sleep or recited the proverbs of Solomon as he helped them with the household chores. No doubt the words from Moses' writings and the prophecies of Isaiah and others were familiar to the young boy as he grew under their tutelage. Day after day, year after year, they transmitted the legacy of faith in words and in actions.

When Paul first visited Lystra (Acts 16:1), it was clear that God had planted the seed of faith in Timothy and opened his heart to the message of salvation. Because of the faithful work of his mother and grandmother as tender teachers of the truth, Timothy was ready to go with Paul on his missionary journeys, to preach the Word, and tell the Good News of the Savior.

If we desire our children and grandchildren to know and love God, then we would do well to follow the example of Lois and Eunice. From our little ones' earliest days we are to be teaching them Scripture, singing spiritual songs, and telling them Bible stories. Through the Word, the Holy Spirit will build a foundation from which they can be prepared to live as God's children and to tell others of God's love.

Scripture for Further Meditation:
Only be careful, and watch yourselves closely so that you do not forget the things your eyes have seen or let them slip from your heart as long as you live. Teach them to your children and to their children after them. Deuteronomy 4:9

$\mathscr{P}rayer$:

I thank You, Jesus, for the rich legacy of faith You have given in Your Word. Help me this day to teach Your truth to my children and grandchildren so they might grow in Your love and in wisdom and knowledge of You so they might also be witnesses for You. Amen.

The Chain of Motherhood

Likewise, teach the older women to be reverent in the way they live, not to be slanderers or addicted to much wine, but to teach what is good. Then they can train the younger women to love their husbands and children, to be self-controlled and pure, to be busy at home, to be kind, and to be subject to their husbands so that no one will malign the word of God. Titus 2:3–5

For a period of three years we attended a military chapel located on a large naval station. We enjoyed the fellowship of other believers and were involved in Bible study and chapel activities. Although there was a great spirit of youth and enthusiasm, there was something missing in this congregation. There were no senior citizens in regular attendance.

In Scripture we are often reminded to learn from the experiences of those who have walked with the Lord for many years. They have a life-perspective that allows them to see things from the vantage point of time. How will this play out in the long run? What issues will remain important and which ones will not matter? Or as one seasoned Christian once told me, "Trust me, honey, this is *not* the hill you want to die on!" Without the insights of those who have walked before us in the pathway of faith, we often lack the vision we need.

Paul affirmed this truth as he wrote to Titus and the believers on the Isle of Crete. In order for the body of Christ to function at its best, the members who are mature need to share their wisdom with those who lack experience. This process requires, then, that the younger and more inexperienced members be willing to learn and profit from the teaching of their elders. As ideal as this process sounds, our pride can sometimes be a barrier to it.

If I, as an older mother, choose to be a poor example of Christianity by my attitude or actions, I limit my positive influence on others. Or if I, as a younger mother, choose to be too proud to submit to the teaching and example of those who are older and wiser, I lose out on a rich resource for strength and encouragement. Mothers of all ages are to submit to the Lordship of Christ in order for this chain of mothering to benefit all. There is no room for condemnation or criticism of one another. Together with other mothers of all ages we can learn and grow and ultimately become examples of motherhood for the unbelieving world in which we live. For our ultimate goal is, as Paul states, "that no one will malign the word of God."

Scripture for Further Meditation:
But encourage one another daily, as long as it is called Today, so that none of you may be hardened by sin's deceitfulness.
Hebrews 3:13

Prayer:

Thank You, God, for my church family.
Help me to have an open heart to learn
from those older than I, and a humble heart
to teach those who are younger. Under
Your loving guidance may we all grow up
together in You. Amen.

Chosen to Be a Mother

To the chosen lady and her children, whom
I love in the truth—and not I only, but also
all who know the truth—because of the truth
which lives in us and will be with us forever.
2 John 1–2

Biblical scholars believe that this short epistle from John is addressed to an individual, but may also be intended for a congregation of believers. The lady spoken of in verse 1 could, in the second instance, be a metaphor for a local church. While we do not know for certain which was John's intent, this small book provides a perfect summary for any devotional book about mothers as it emphasizes three key principles that guide us as Christians.

First is the principle that all godly living depends upon knowing the truth—the Truth, which is Jesus Christ. When we have a personal relationship with Jesus, our children and grandchildren should see it reflected in our lives: time spent daily in the Scriptures, prayer with our Lord, and worship with other believers. And the Holy Spirit, who brought us to faith, will continue to provide us with strength and encouragement.

Second is the principle that when we know the truth as revealed in Scripture, the Holy Spirit will empower us to live out our lives in loving obedience to Him (see verse 6). Children learn by observing others. When our children and grandchildren see us act with kindness, they will be encouraged to be kind. When we confess our sins, they will learn that they can ask God to forgive them—and that they can forgive others with God's help. If, however, we worry and nag, they will only learn anxiety and mistrust. Through the power of the Spirit, we can increasingly speak and act in ways that model God's love to our sons and daugthers.

Third is the principle that continuing in the truth guards us from following false teaching (see verse 9). There will always be those who invent new ways to "find God," "discover the meaning of life," or "have a deeper experience." By saturating ourselves in God's Word, the Spirit will enable us to discern for ourselves and our children if these new ideas are true or false. The closer we are to the true Light, the clearer God reveals things around us. As mothers we are to be aware of what the world is teaching our children and by God's help teach them to distinguish what is truth and what is a lie.

As chosen mothers, daughters of God, we have available the comfort and help of the Holy Spirit not only to learn the truth, but also to walk in it and teach it to our children. What an awesome privilege this is! How wonderful to know that Jesus Christ is constantly with us in this adventure of mothering.

Scripture for Further Meditation:
May God Himself, the God of peace,
sanctify you through and through.
May your whole spirit, soul and body
be kept blameless at the coming of our
Lord Jesus Christ. The one who calls
you is faithful and He will do it.
1 Thessalonians 5:23–24

Prayer:

Dear Jesus, I thank You for the privilege
of being a mother. Help me to follow You
in the paths of truth so I may instruct and
lead my children in Your way so they may
walk more closely with You. May my life
always bring glory to Your name. Amen.

DATE DUE